THE REAL READER'S QUARTERLY

Slightly Foxed

'Accepting an Invitation'

NO.64   WINTER 2019

Editors Gail Pirkis & Hazel Wood

Marketing and publicity Stephanie Allen & Jennie Harrison Bunning

Bookshops Anna Kirk

Subscriptions Hattie Summers & Jess Dalby

Cover illustration: Seren Bell, 'Winter Cockerel'

Seren Bell was brought up deep in the Devonshire countryside and now lives in the beautiful Wye valley on the Welsh borders. Her work, in pen, ink and crayon, is concerned with the animals that are part of our rural heritage and reflects her love for them and the landscape in which she walks every day. More of her work can be seen at www.fossegallery.com.

Design by Octavius Murray

Layout by Andrew Evans

Colophon, tailpiece and back cover fox by David Eccles

Published by Slightly Foxed Limited
53 Hoxton Square
London NI 6PB

tel 020 7033 0258
email office@foxedquarterly.com
www.foxedquarterly.com

Slightly Foxed is published quarterly in early March, June, September and December

Annual subscription rates (4 issues)
UK and Ireland £48; Overseas £56

Single copies of this issue can be bought for £12.50 (UK) or £14.50 (Overseas)

All back issues in printed form are also available

ISBN 978-1-910898-37-6
ISSN 1742-5794

Printed and bound by Smith Settle, Yeadon, West Yorkshire

Contents

Contents

John Watson

The Slightly Foxed Podcast

A new episode of our podcast is available on the 15th of every month. To listen, visit www.foxedquarterly.com/pod or search for Slightly Foxed on Audioboom, iTunes or your podcast app.

Subscriber Benefits

Slightly Foxed can obtain any books reviewed in this issue, whether new or second-hand. To enquire about a book, to access the digital edition of *Slightly Foxed* or to view a list of membership benefits, visit www.foxedquarterly.com/ members or contact the office: 020 7033 0258/office@foxedquarterly.com.

From the Editors

Was there ever a moment when a good book seemed more essential? And not just because Christmas and the annual search for presents has come round again. Comfort, instruction, amusement, escape, a new perspective – whatever it is you're looking for as a steadier in unnerving times, it's all there in books.

This winter's new Slightly Foxed Edition is certainly a lifter of spirits and an escape route to what feels like a freer and more straightforward world. Following on from his childhood memoir *Boy*, which we published in the autumn, *Going Solo* (see p. 13) is Roald Dahl's invigorating and often very amusing account of working for Shell in the country then called Tanganyika, travelling the dirt roads to visit the eccentric expatriates who literally kept the machinery of Empire running. The second half of the book takes on a somewhat darker tone, as war breaks out and Dahl drives the 600 miles to Nairobi to enlist as a fighter pilot and subsequently take part in the RAF's heroic defence of Greece. It's a young man's story, bold, stomach-churning and brilliantly told, all overlaid with Dahl's irrepressible determination, optimism and humour.

At this time of year we don't need to remind you that the winter *Slightly Foxed* catalogue is full of ideas for presents to suit all tastes, not to mention our traditional literary Christmas crossword. But we would like to draw your attention to something rather special this year: the Slightly Foxed Revolving Bookcase. Made to order in oak or ash at Dominic and Arabella Parish's Wardour Workshops in Wiltshire, and designed to hold around 90 Slightly Foxed Editions or books of similar size, it is an elegant modern take on the traditional revolving bookcases which were so much a feature of Victorian and Edwardian homes; and it's both useful and decorative. Inevitably an original piece like this comes at a price, but if you do happen to be on the lookout for a very special present for someone bookish, or even a special (and very practical) treat for yourself, you would be supporting real craftsmen and commissioning something truly lasting.

And while we're on the subject of independent businesses, we've said it before and we'll say it again: please this Christmas, if you can, support your local bookshop. We've recently learned of the demise of one of our favourites – Wenlock Books in the lovely Shropshire town of Much Wenlock – which had been there for 30 years, largely killed off by the online giant. Small really is beautiful, we believe.

It's almost a year now since we started the *Slightly Foxed* podcasts. After initial nerves about exposing ourselves on air (Hazel still fears she sounds like recordings of the Queen *circa* 1950), we're enjoying this new way of being in touch. We've learned from some fascinating guests about a range of subjects, from the art of biography to the history of garden writing, and judging from the letters and press mentions we've received, many people look forward to these monthly glimpses of life here at *SF*. We're already lining up a selection of interesting guests for the coming year. We do hope you'll join us.

Meantime we send you our very best wishes for a peaceful Christmas and an optimistic 2020.

GAIL PIRKIS & HAZEL WOOD

Accepting an Invitation

DAISY HAY

My grandfather Jack Mackenzie-Stuart was a man of immense learning and eclectic tastes. He collected eighteenth-century French drawings, loved jazz and hated opera. He gave me hardback editions of *The Oxford Book of English Verse* and *Alice's Adventures in Wonderland* and on my eighth birthday offered me a £10 bribe to learn by heart sonnets by Shakespeare, Wordsworth and Keats. He took me to the Ashmolean Museum in Oxford to teach me about perspective in front of Uccello's *The Hunt in the Forest* and he kept a video of *Meet Me in St Louis* in his study for family emergencies.

The Christmas I was 11 he gave me an audio cassette of Joyce Grenfell reading her autobiography, *Joyce Grenfell Requests the Pleasure*. I didn't know who Joyce Grenfell was and showed it to my mother in some puzzlement. She wondered aloud if he'd meant to give me a cassette of Joyce Grenfell performing her monologues. I was already a fan of Flanders and Swann – whose recordings my grandfather had given me a year earlier – so this seemed possible. Monologues or no monologues, the post-Christmas car journey from Edinburgh back to Oxford was still six hours long and the time had to be filled somehow. So I slotted the first tape into my Walkman and heard Joyce's crisp tones saying this:

> The background to my mother is light. All the rooms she lived in were light. Pale rooms with notes of strong colour: geranium-

---

Joyce Grenfell, *Joyce Grenfell Requests the Pleasure* (1976) is out of print but we can obtain second-hand copies.

pink, 'lipstick'-red, chalk-blue, saffron-yellow. No top lighting; pools of light from lamps with wide white shades painted pink inside, to her order; pools of light on tables. Low bowls of massed, solid-coloured flowers: geraniums, primroses, gardenias, roses.

Joyce took me all the way from Edinburgh to Oxford that Christmas. In the process she also transported me to 1920s Cliveden and wartime London and across the Middle East. I found half her references incomprehensible, but it didn't seem to matter. By the time we got home I was a paid-up devotee.

This summer I found my grandfather's edition of *Joyce Grenfell Requests the Pleasure* sitting on the bookshelves of his study. He has been dead for eighteen years now, but his books remain undisturbed in the house he loved and I found Joyce sitting between a three-volume treatise on legal history and a copy of Nancy Mitford's *The Sun King*. Reading (rather than listening) for the first time, I'm no longer surprised that the audiobook made such an impression on me. When Joyce started writing radio reviews for the *Observer* in 1937 the paper's editor, J. L. Garvin, told her approvingly that she had 'the flick of the wrist in writing'. He was absolutely right. Her writing style is as clipped and precise as her accent and she has the knack in *Requests the Pleasure* of capturing people with a few brisk strokes. Her mother shimmers in pink sitting-rooms; her father is 'a confidence-restorer . . . a big man who stood firm'. Her powerful aunt Nancy Astor strides through the pages dressed in golf clothes and chewing gum. Joyce writes of Aunt Nancy with gratitude and affection but skewers her all the same with a single sentence: 'She rarely listened, she only told.'

Joyce Grenfell was born in 1910. *Requests the Pleasure* was published in 1976 and takes her as far as the opening of her first solo show in 1954. Her story begins in a world of Edwardian nannies and awkward adolescent girls, affecting fashions she has fun in gently ridiculing. 'I see us now,' she writes of herself and her friends,

> our peculiar Twenties figures forced flat by bust-bodices, made from lengths of stout satin ribbon twelve inches wide . . . We do not use rouge or eye-pencil, but have discovered Tangee lipstick that is supposed to take on our own natural colour, but which stains our lips light purple. Our face-powder is no longer pink but honey-beige. We compare notes about this, and about deodorants that don't make us itch and hair-removers that do the job but smell horrible, of rotting vegetation.

This passage epitomizes one of the particular charms of *Requests the Pleasure*, namely that Joyce understands that people live in bodies and that biographies that fail to take account of this don't fully animate their subjects. With her eye firmly on the absurd details of living she is able to bring to life grand ceremonies and set pieces. The first time she wears her hair up in public she is at the Paris opera house and the sound of falling hairpins punctuates the evening's music. When she gets married the square neck of the dress she has set her heart on in the face of maternal opposition fails to sit flat, 'but after all it was my wedding and I knew what I wanted'.

Although Joyce had plenty of grand relations, money after her marriage at 19 to Reggie Grenfell was tight. They lived in a cottage on the Cliveden estate, lent by formidable Aunt Nancy in exchange for Joyce's services as substitute stay-at-home daughter. Radio reviewing thus provided a valuable additional income of £10 a week. She writes happily of remembering her disbelief that someone was prepared to pay her for doing the two things she liked best: writing and listening to the radio. In January 1939 she was invited to dinner by the radio producer Stephen Potter and after dinner she gave a spoof

Women's Institute lecture on 'Useful and Acceptable Gifts'. One of her fellow guests was the theatrical director Herbert Farjeon who was sufficiently impressed by what he'd heard to cajole Joyce into appearing as a guest in his next West End revue.

Joyce tells the story of her theatrical debut as a series of happy accidents. This allows her to present herself as a fortunate amateur, marvelling at the strange subculture of the stage. Her biographer Janie Hampton has sensitively debunked the serendipity of her debut, revealing that in reality Joyce was highly focused and ambitious in her pursuit of wider recognition. The story of the accidental performer isn't disingenuous though. Instead it's one of the ways Joyce takes her reader into her confidence, so that you feel she is talking just to you. Her writing style is deceptively familiar and she shows herself at work. 'My mind goes blank when I read descriptions of people's looks,' she confesses. 'I just cannot see those dancing eyes and mouths too wide for beauty that novelists used to give their tousle-headed heroines.'

Joyce performed in the West End until the Blitz shut down the London theatres. On the day war broke out she had been handed two evacuees as she left the house for the theatre where she performed in front of a minute audience who made 'as much noise as they could; in fact they worked harder than we did'. For a period she combined voluntary nursing at the Red Cross hospital installed at Cliveden with performing and radio reviewing, before being called up to join the Entertainments National Service Association, or ENSA. The longest and best section of *Requests the Pleasure* tells the story of Joyce's war service with ENSA. Between January 1944 and March 1945 she travelled with the pianist Viola Tunnard to fourteen countries on two separate tours. Their brief was to entertain troops in hospitals and units in hard-to-reach places that could not be served by larger companies. They performed in North Africa, Malta, Italy, Iraq and India, contending with battlefields, overwhelmed casualty stations, errant mice and bad pianos.

Joyce is careful to put her own service in the context of the greater sacrifices made by the soldiers and nursing staff she encountered, but despite the bleak conditions and suffering she describes she is always alive to the prospect of comedy. In India she and Viola find themselves announced as 'two well-known artistes who have been flown

out from home to entertain the men in bed', to the great pleasure of a waiting ward of injured soldiers. Elsewhere she writes feelingly of the variety of plumbing arrangements in their digs. 'Both of us were put off by the absence of sitting equipment,' she recalls. 'We far preferred quite long walks across the desert to canvas-walled privies, open to the skies . . . usually arranged companionably in separate pairs.'

Joyce returned home in 1945 to join the cast of Noël Coward's new review, *Sigh No More*. From then on she became an increasingly well-known stage and radio performer, and she vividly evokes the theatrical world of post-war London, in which egos clash and fashions slowly change. She describes finding her voice as a writer and reveals the genesis of some of her best-known characters, including the harassed nursery teacher of 'George', who today remains her most famous creation. She writes of her mother's regret that her film appearances (principally as the hapless Ruby Gates in the St Trinian's series) were so resolutely gawky: couldn't she once, 'just for *once*, now and then, look a little less unglamorous'? Elsewhere she concedes disarmingly, 'I have never minded looking funny – when it was intentional.'

Reading *Joyce Grenfell Requests the Pleasure* this summer, the memory of my first acquaintance with her has been strong. I've heard the precise tones and emphases of her own reading in every line and I've realized what I didn't before, namely that her story offers a wonderfully detailed and idiosyncratic account of life between the wars in Britain. Her narrative is punctuated with well-known names, but above all it offers a vivid sense of what it was like to inhabit a body at a particular point in time. Some of the attitudes and sentiments feel dated now and Joyce is frank about the difficult experience of looking at her younger self and not entirely liking what she sees. Her liking for life is evident throughout though, and her autobiography offers an excellent introduction both to her own work and to the lost world in which she learnt her craft.

As well as Joyce's voice, on this rereading I've also heard in her story my grandfather's voice. While she was entertaining the troops in the Middle East he was defusing bombs and building bridges in Belgium and Holland as a young Royal Engineer. Like her he had to return to post-war Britain and work out how to make a meaningful life in a country that felt at once familiar and strange. I now realize why he thought I should listen to her story. She shows that it is possible to make a living doing the thing one likes most and also that there are interesting and extraordinary things to be found in the most unexpected places. I have my grandfather's wartime letters on my desk, and I see that in 1943, during a convalescence at a military hospital in Kent, he sent his mother a sketch of the ceiling frieze above his bed, simply because it was beautiful and interesting. No wonder he accepted the invitation to look at the world through Joyce Grenfell's sympathetic eyes with such pleasure. All these years later I am very glad he extended the invitation to me too.

DAISY HAY is currently writing about the eighteenth-century publisher Joseph Johnson, another figure who found interesting things in unexpected places and was generous and hospitable to all-comers. Her most recent book is *The Making of Mary Shelley's Frankenstein*.

A Master of Invention

HENRY JEFFREYS

We were fortunate, those of us who grew up in the 1980s. Almost every year there would be a new book by Roald Dahl which would be passed around at school and discussed with great seriousness. There were also playground arguments about his name: 'It's not Ronald, it's Roald! Don't you know anything?'

We lived in Dahl's world, my brother and I more literally than most children since we grew up a couple of miles from Gypsy House, his home in Great Missenden. As we drove past it my parents would always say: 'That's where Roald Dahl lives.' I think I used to doubt them. Could Dahl really live somewhere as prosaic as an ordinary house in rural Buckinghamshire? I liked to think he lived in a Willy Wonka-style factory turning out madcap books with the help of oompa loompas. I met him once at a charity event; he was sitting at a table looking very old and signing books.

When *Boy*, Dahl's memoir of his schooldays, was published in 1984 (see *SF* no. 63), it had a powerful effect on my class. It felt as if he was talking to us directly. When the sequel, *Going Solo*, appeared in 1986, I took it out of the school library and read it cover to cover in one sitting. *Going Solo* picks up where *Boy* left off, in 1936 with Dahl now an adult, sailing to East Africa to work for Shell.

The first thing that struck me when I reread it all these years later was how very like his stories his own life was. On the long voyage to Africa, the elderly couple who run around the boat naked or the man who pretends to have dandruff so nobody will suspect that he wears a wig seem to have stepped from the pages of Dahl's children's books. One can picture them drawn by Quentin Blake. The animals too: he describes elephants, 'their skin hung loose over their bodies like suits they had inherited from larger ancestors, with the trousers ridiculously baggy', while vultures are 'feathered undertakers'.

Later in the book, there's an incident with a rogue lion: 'Come quick! Come quick! A huge lion is eating the wife of the cook!' The mixture of the comic and the tragic reminded me of the beginning of *James and the Giant Peach* where James's parents are killed by a rhinoceros which has escaped from London Zoo.

If these incidents feel as if they've sprung from Dahl's imagination it's probably because they had. *Going Solo* is largely based on long letters that Dahl wrote to his adored mother, Sofie Magdalene, in England. Dahl's biographer, Donald Sturrock, thought that 'Most of these delightful characters were almost certainly invented as an entertaining alternative to his real companions on the journey who were dismissed in a letter home as "pretty dull".'

So *Going Solo* is not a memoir in any conventional sense of the word. Just as in *Boy*, it is Dahl telling stories loosely based on his life for the benefit of children. The Dahl of *Going Solo* is a curious Peter Pan-like figure experiencing adult adventures without growing up properly. Apart from a hint of romance when he is in hospital in Alexandria after a plane crash, there is no hint of sex in the book, which is just how we liked it. Dahl's great gift was that he related to children better than to adults. A friend of my parents knew him and told me that though he could be difficult with adults, he always had time for their daughter and used to make up elaborate nicknames for her.

We loved Dahl because he shared our impatience and confusion with the adult world. In *Going Solo*, the adults are the British. Despite being born and raised in Wales and England, Dahl was an outsider. He spoke Norwegian at home and only got his first British passport when he went abroad with Shell. Here is Dahl the anthropologist:

In the 1930s, the British Empire was still very much the British Empire, and the men and women who kept it going were a race of people that most of you have never encountered and now you never will. I consider myself very lucky to have caught a glimpse of this rare species while it still roamed the forests and foothills of the earth.

In Africa his closest relationship is with his manservant Mdisho, whose boyishness (he was 19) is contrasted with the stuffiness of the British. When war breaks out, Mdisho, full of martial enthusiasm, beheads a German sisal owner, 'a very wealthy and extremely unpleasant bachelor', with Dahl's antique sword. Again, this incident almost certainly never happened. Mdisho exists not as a caricature of Africans but as the child in the book baffled by adult ways. And as always with Dahl, death and violence are dealt with unsentimentally.

Later, Dahl's confusion with the British turned into contempt for his senior officers and the general amateurishness of the war effort. 'This, I told myself, is a waste of manpower and machinery,' he writes at one point on the token British fighter presence in Greece. Despite being 6 ft 6 in, he trained as a fighter pilot. We are on slightly firmer ground with the RAF years. There are no doubt embellishments here and there but much of what he wrote can be corroborated. Dahl was a superb pilot; he passed third out of 40 in his intake, and in his brief career had a number of confirmed kills. His descriptions of an air battle in his Hurricane is mesmerizing: 'I was quite literally overwhelmed by the feeling that I had been into the very bowels of the fiery furnace and had managed to claw my way out.'

This love of flying recurs throughout Dahl's work. It's there in *James and the Giant Peach* or *Charlie and the Chocolate Factory*. Indeed, Dahl's first foray into writing was an account of his crash in the Libyan desert early in his RAF career. It's a story he told many times. In some versions he is shot down, but in *Going Solo* he is given the wrong co-ordinates of the base he is making for in North Africa and, with night closing in and running out of fuel, he is forced to make a crash landing in the desert.

What is certain is that he suffered severe head and back injuries and was very nearly killed. In *Going Solo* he writes of undergoing 'sixteen major operations on numerous parts of my body' and spending four months convalescing in hospital in Alexandria. He did fly again but suffered from severe back pain for the rest of his life. He thought, however, that the crash also changed him mentally and made him a writer.

Dahl first began writing short stories for adults that were extremely popular in America and it was only in 1961 that he wrote *James and the Giant Peach*. In his lifetime, his children's books were hated by some librarians, but Dahl knew his audience: 'a grown-up talking about a children's book is like a man talking about a woman's hat'.

Going Solo appeared towards the end of an extraordinarily fertile patch in his career when, with the support of his second wife, Felicity Crosland, and a collaborative editor at Farrar, Straus and Giroux, Stephen Roxburgh, he wrote classics like *The BFG* and *Matilda*, with vivid illustrations by Quentin Blake.

Roald Dahl died in 1990. Since then his personal reputation has taken a bit of a battering. He clearly had a temper and could be extremely unpleasant. And yet, for me, that doesn't dent the magic of the books. Rereading *Going Solo*, I was struck by his powers as a storyteller: humour, economy, a vivid eye for detail, and that uncanny ability to talk directly to his reader. One of my happiest moments was hearing my daughter's fits of giggles the first time I read her *The BFG*.

My parents still live near Great Missenden. One day a couple of years ago, my daughter was feeding the ducks behind the Red Lion, not far from Gypsy House (which is now a museum), when she made friends with two girls who were doing the same. Their mother looked strangely familiar. It was Sophie Dahl, the inspiration for *The BFG*, and those little girls were Roald Dahl's great-grandchildren. The girls and the ducks took on a Quentin Blake-like quality, and Roald Dahl's presence suddenly felt palpable.

HENRY JEFFREYS is a drinks writer based in south London. One day he will return to rural Buckinghamshire and prop up the bar at the Red Lion but not quite yet.

Roald Dahl's *Going Solo* (236pp) is now available in a limited and numbered cloth-bound edition of 2,000 copies (subscribers: UK & Eire £17, Overseas £19; non-subscribers: UK & Eire £18.50, Overseas £20.50). All prices include post and packing. Copies may be ordered by post (53 Hoxton Square, London N1 6PB), by phone (020 7033 0258) or via our website www.foxedquarterly.com.

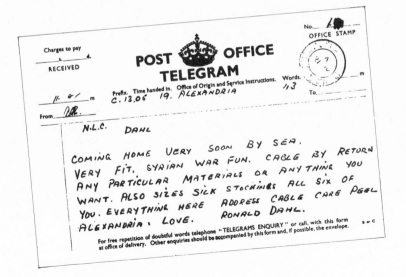

Thames Valley Blues

CHRIS SAUNDERS

Patrick Hamilton, now best known for his novel *Hangover Square* and the play *Gaslight*, was a troubled man who is often seen as the court poet of shabby alcoholics and wandering drunkards. He is, however, also the bard of a particular area west of London, that part of the Thames valley that extends from just beyond Slough to Reading, where his characters often go to seek refuge from the excesses of the city. This is a strange hinterland of pretty villages and small towns occupied largely by people who work in London, places that are eerily quiet during the week (apart from the air traffic from Heathrow, which of course Hamilton knew nothing about) and yet vitally attached to the metropolis. I know this area well because it's where I grew up – a train ride away from London and yet irredeemably, parochially South Bucks.

Hamilton's bitter-sweet wartime novel *The Slaves of Solitude* (1947) expresses the semi-detached insularity of these places better than any other book I know. The fictional town in which the book is set, Thames Lockdon – how close that word is to 'lockdown' – is based on Henley, the quintessential Thames valley river town. It is a measure of the slow pace of progress in such a place that Hamilton cites as the most glamorous local nightclub Skindles in Maidenhead, a real-life venue also beloved of Evelyn Waugh that was still open and alluring in the mid-1980s when I attended a twelfth birthday party there.

Hamilton's heroine Enid Roach, a 39-year-old spinster always

Patrick Hamilton, *The Slaves of Solitude* (1947)
Abacus · Pb · 368pp · £9.99 · ISBN 9780349141541

known as Miss Roach, has moved to Thames Lockdon to avoid the
Blitz, but she travels back to her publishing job in London every day.
The opening passage of the book expresses beautifully and brutally
the interdependence of city and suburb, and makes clear Miss Roach's
plight:

> London, the crouching monster, like every other monster has
> to breathe, and breathe it does in its own obscure, malignant
> way. Its vital oxygen is composed of suburban working men
> and women of all kinds, who every morning are sucked up
> through an infinitely complicated respiratory apparatus of
> trains and termini into the mighty congested lungs, held there
> for a number of hours, and then, in the evening, exhaled vio-
> lently through the same channels.

You would think that Thames Lockdon would represent an escape,
and Hamilton does present its prettiness, the beauty of its surrounding
countryside and its friendliness as an antidote to the aggravations of
the city. Yet, as anyone who has ever lived in a small town can attest,
knowing everybody and their business brings pressures of its own.

Miss Roach lodges at the Rosamund Tea Rooms, a community in
miniature that is presided over by the tyrannical Mr Thwaites, a brilliant comic character who represents every parochial boor who ever
wrote a mean-spirited semi-literate letter to the local paper. He speaks
in an almost surreally pompous patois of jocularity, archaism and sly
innuendo – for instance upon hearing Miss Roach is going to meet
her German friend Vicki Kugelmann for coffee:

> 'She goeth, perchance, unto the coffee house,' said Mr Thwaites,
> 'there to partake of the noxious brown fluid with her continental
> friends?'

The accusatory inference in the words 'continental friends' is
unmistakable. This is, after all, wartime, and Vicki is therefore a

suspicious character. However, as far as Mr Thwaites is concerned, all foreigners are suspicious. The Russians also count as Miss Roach's 'friends', because she once pointed out how important they are as allies, and so she is simultaneously a Nazi sympathizer and a communist fellow traveller. Anything beyond the bounds of the Rosamund Tea Rooms is used as a stick to beat her with, even more so when the Americans come to town. Miss Roach finds herself in a half-baked relationship with the diffident Lieutenant Pike, an airman from a local base, and the exoticism of 'our Democratic friends from across the Atlantic' is almost too much for Mr Thwaites's prurience to bear.

Hamilton has rather wonderfully set up two opposing types of Britishness in Roach and Thwaites. The metropolitan Miss Roach prides herself on her liberalism and fair-mindedness, even though privately she finds Vicki irritatingly affected and the Lieutenant frustratingly inconsequential. Ranged against her is Mr Thwaites, whose personality is made up entirely of unprocessed imperialist attitudes and snobberies and yet who takes Vicki to his heart. So shallow are his opinions that when Vicki moves into the Rosamund Tea Rooms, he falls pathetically in love with her continental otherness. Together, they conspire to make life unbearable for Miss Roach. Vicki plays with the loyalties of the inconstant Lieutenant Pike by deliberately outshining the reserved Miss Roach, while Mr Thwaites casts aspersions on her totally innocent relationship with the 17-year-old son of a friend. Everything that Miss Roach values about her own kind of Britishness – her decency, kindness and moderation – is turned against her.

It is in these circumstances that London becomes the place of escape, despite the ravages of war. Another inhabitant of the Rosamund Tea Rooms, Mr Prest, is a semi-retired comic actor who is deemed rather vulgar by his fellow guests. He finds himself work in the Wimbledon pantomime and invites Miss Roach to a performance. In the most joyous sequence in the book the transformation she sees in him also works magic upon her. All the drabness of Thames Lockdon is spirited away by his appearance as a comic uncle:

> Here he was, with a whole house of children screaming at him . . . dancing, singing, falling, getting into difficulties with his trousers, exultantly triumphing! . . . Somehow his triumph seemed to be Miss Roach's triumph as well, and her heart was lifted up with pleasure.

Whatever the dangers of the Blitz, London seems to be a place of vitality, excitement and anonymous refuge. Mr Prest finds joy in the guise of a pantomime uncle while Miss Roach discovers pleasure in the anonymity of the crowd.

My own upbringing in the Thames valley was rather less dramatic than Miss Roach's experience, but I recognize this vision of London as a kind of Shangri-La. Slough in the 1980s was no more exciting, and much less pretty, than the Thames Lockdon of Hamilton's imagination. I moved to London as soon as I could after university to pursue the same kind of vibrant, cosmopolitan life that Miss Roach seeks. When, to her surprise, she inherits a fortune and moves to Claridge's, I experience a sympathetic thrill of relief and pleasure. However, *The Slaves of Solitude* would not be a Patrick Hamilton novel if it did not contain a salutary message.

No sooner has Miss Roach moved into Claridge's than she is worrying whether it really suits her. The luxury intimidates her, because she is modest, unassuming, thrifty, 'not the sort of person to go in for double rooms at places like Claridge's'. The novel ends with her lying in one of the hotel's wonderfully comfortable beds musing on having to find somewhere to live, going back to work and hoping for the best. In other words, she is looking forward to returning to her normal, quiet life, rather than escaping into a world of opulent dreams. It is all very well running to London from the suffocation of small-town life, but you bring with you the same basic desires that you had all along. There is no escape from your own personality, and that is why Miss Roach is always complaining about everything she has. She still hasn't found her home.

We don't know where Enid Roach goes after this. The novel ends by giving her a fresh start, which you feel is the real reward for her decency and integrity, rather than the inheritance itself. The last line of the novel is a blessing upon every reader: 'God help us, God help all of us, every one, all of us', as we are sent off with the hope of avoiding the bombs on the one hand and the barbs on the other.

Above all, it is an injunction to live honestly and kindly. At the very beginning of the novel, Hamilton showed us that London is a monster, which was a pretty good clue that it would never be the answer to Miss Roach's needs. After ten years of living in the disinterested jumble of London, I came to the same conclusion. I now live in a different small town, a place of friendship and common spirit. While I still commute to the capital most days, I no longer see London as the promised land. I have found my corner of Britain, and I hope Miss Roach has found hers.

CHRIS SAUNDERS is managing director of the antiquarian bookseller Henry Sotheran Ltd. He also writes and runs his own blog, SpeaksVolumes.

Playing it for Laughs

AMANDA THEUNISSEN

You read a book, laugh a lot, recommend it to your friends. Some laugh, others don't. Why is a sense of humour so individual and at the same time so culturally specific? We are mostly moved to the same emotional responses by tragedy, but we don't laugh at the same things and I've always wondered why. There are many kinds of humour and life would be intolerable without it, but as society changes, so humour changes too. We still weep at old Greek tragedies – but laugh at old Greek comedies? Not so much.

So it's a rare treat to find comic books written a while ago that still work. In the 1940s two wonderful writers called Caryl Brahms and S. J. Simon collaborated on two such novels. Their aim was to make people laugh when there was nothing much to laugh at, and if ever those kinds of books were needed, it's now. The two had written successful comic detective stories like *Bullet in the Ballet* before the war, but *Don't, Mr Disraeli!* (1940) and *No Bed for Bacon* (1941) were their first highly unreliable rearrangements of British history. They were very funny then and are very funny now, at least I think so.

I inherited my 1963 copy of *Don't, Mr Disraeli!* from my father. It's a retelling of *Romeo and Juliet* transferred to a glorious Victorian age that never existed, though one wishes it had. It is totally inconsequential: I can't even begin to explain the plot, not that it matters. The basis is the feud between the middle-class Clutterwick and Shuttleforth families, and what happens when Julian Clutterwick (who

---

Caryl Brahms and S. J. Simon, *Don't, Mr Disraeli!* (1940) and *No Bed for Bacon* (1941), are both out of print but we can obtain second-hand copies.

looks just like John Gielgud) and Julia Shuttleforth ('I'd forget him more easily if he didn't look so like John Gielgud') fall in love and want to marry.

That's just the start. Threads of other stories criss-cross, peopled by credulous uncles, ferocious aunts, observant crossing sweepers, armies of loyal servants, a scheming French governess and all sorts of running gags that don't advance the plot, such as it is, but are an essential element of the fun. The authors are much given to addressing the reader directly, particularly when so deeply embroiled that a resolution seems impossible. It could be called post-modernism, but I'm sure Brahms and Simon just thought it was a good joke.

Everything is in the melting pot. Time is definitely fluid, ushering in a cast of hundreds, including Victoria herself at whatever age suits the exigencies of the story, and the eponymous Mr Disraeli, his behaviour and ideas earning the reproof of the title. I can't do better than quote the authors' own 'Explanation':

This is not a novel set in the Victorian Age; it is a novel set in its literature . . . and any event in this period may come into focus, bearing no relation to the date at which it happened. This treaty with time has enabled the authors to prolong the lives of some famous men and women and allow others to live before they have yet been born and introduce some beloved giants from our own age.

So anachronistic figures drift in and out, including Noël Coward, George Gershwin, Henry James, Compton Mackenzie, James Agate and assorted members of the Savage Club, as well as the book's publisher, Michael Joseph (so mean with his advances and advertising), and Albert Einstein and his father, always worrying about Albert's obsession with numbers.

The Marx Brothers play a large part, Harpo chasing terrified blondes whenever more mayhem is needed. The moustachioed villain,

Daniel Macklin

much given to cracking his whip while evicting widows and orphans and trying to seduce our heroine, is clearly Groucho. The plot demands that he murder one of the credulous uncles. 'A capital scheme, decides our villain, he will make a rendezvous forthwith. He reaches for the telephone. Curses! It will not be invented for another thirty years.'

Who were the authors known as Brahms and Simon? Both were Jewish and their fantastical lives read like something from their own books. Caryl, born and bred in Croydon (her grandparents were Turkish Sephardic immigrants), was christened Doris Caroline Abrahams and was destined by her parents to be a concert pianist. However, being, as she said, a natural critic, she couldn't bear the noise she made, so changed her name to Caryl Brahms (which she thought gender neutral) and reinvented herself as a ballet critic and comic writer.

S. J. Simon, born Seca Jaca Skidelsky in Manchuria in 1900, arrived in England as a child. Universally known as Skid, he was a journalist and writer, but until the success of *Don't, Mr Disraeli!* he earned his living teaching bridge: he was a world-class international player. He died in 1948 and his obituaries mistakenly called Caryl his wife, but they weren't even lovers. They were friends and collaborators for twenty years, producing twelve books, plays, revue songs, captions for strip cartoons – and they swore at the end of each one that they would never join forces again. In her diary Caryl wrote: 'Finished DMD today. Emptied an ashtray over Skid's head, been longing to do it for ages.'

After his death, Caryl wrote on her own until 1954 when she met Ned Sherrin, the TV producer and writer, who became her second and last collaborator. She was happier working in a team, always maintaining she was not witty herself but the cause of wit in others.

Don't, Mr Disraeli! was Brahms and Simon's first major success – an old lady wrote claiming to clearly remember an incident in it which the authors had invented – and their publisher (the long-suffering Michael Joseph) wanted another book just like it. But repetition wasn't their style and *No Bed for Bacon* was what they came up with. Set in Elizabethan England, it centres on the young Shakespeare and the London theatre world, which they saw as much like the London theatre world they both knew. It's more straightforward than *Don't, Mr Disraeli!* and possibly better written, full of casual learning, unsentimental history and patriotism, and great gaiety. The authors prefaced it with a 'Warning to Scholars: This book is fundamentally unsound.'

My copy is subtitled 'The story of Shakespeare and Lady Viola in love', which is a bit cheeky because it was only added to the new edition – which appeared in 1999, the year of the film *Shakespeare in Love*. In Ned Sherrin's preface he mentions lending his copy to Tom Stoppard before the latter began work on the film's screenplay. Film and book have the same plot – beautiful stage-struck Lady Viola dresses as a boy and gets to act with the young Shakespeare at the Globe; they fall in love but have to part, and all ends slightly sadly.

Substitute *Romeo and Juliet* for *Twelfth Night* and the homage (Sherrin's word) to the novel in the film is clear. But Brahms and Simon present the world of Elizabeth herself, her politics, her court, and of Elizabethan theatre in their own effortless anachronistic style.

Backstage at the Globe Francis Bacon (who is desperate to acquire as an investment one of the many beds the Queen has slept in) is insisting Shakespeare use his, Bacon's, suggestions to improve *Twelfth Night*. The playwright is not happy.

> Shakespeare sprang to his feet. 'Master Bacon,' he demanded passionately, 'do I write my plays or do you?' Bacon looked at him. He shrugged.

Brahms and Simon have fun pushing ideas in the Bard's direction. Want to know how genius works? Amid the backstage chaos of the Globe, Elizabethan clown Obadiah Croke is demanding to play a comic gravedigger; a young actor chips in.

> 'Master Will,' said the boy beseechingly, 'I want to drown myself . . . I wish to go mad . . . and sing wild songs.'
> Shakespeare tasted the idea. 'A mad maid who drowns herself. It's a very good idea.' He tasted it again. 'Dramatic.'
> 'But first,' said the boy, 'I shall need to be betrayed.'

Add the old trouper who yearns to be a groaning ghost, the financial backer's view that most people should die at the end, and with a bit more work on the plot – there you have it: *Hamlet*.

B & S were very conscious of venturing on to hallowed ground with Shakespeare but also understood that not every part of every play is a masterpiece and much of the now incomprehensible Elizabethan humour and wordplay doesn't have to be treated like Holy Writ. My favourite is a really terrible B & S joke that sounds perfectly authentic when told by the court jester:

> Question: What is it that stands on the roof at midnight and
> crows like a cock?
> Answer: A Tom O'Bedlam.

Queen Elizabeth doesn't find it funny – she throws her wig at the hapless courtier who tells it, but as parody it's perfect. It could be inserted seamlessly into Edgar's ravings in *King Lear* or any rustic comedy sequence.

No Bed for Bacon was extremely successful. Even with wartime paper shortages it went into a second printing in a week. One review called it 'irresponsible, irreverent, impudent, and undocumented – one of the soundest books in years'. In her memoirs Caryl Brahms says proudly that they knew the German prisoner-of-war camps established a waiting-list ahead of publication. After the war she met Ronald Searle, a survivor of the Japanese camps, who told her there was always a queue of prisoners asking for the latest B & S.

Rereading the two books yet again, I find new things to laugh at and old friends to greet. But I'm baffled by two characters in *Don't, Mr Disraeli!* There are two critics – one round and podgy, the other dark and cadaverous – who meet every week to exchange carefully honed spontaneous bon mots such as:

'What did you think of the new Ibsen?'
'Bricks without Shaw.'

I'm sure they are real people, carefully described and recognizable, but I can't work out who they are. If any knowledgeable reader can, please put me out of my misery. A postcard c/o *Slightly Foxed* will find me.

AMANDA THEUNISSEN is a television producer who's giving up serious literature for the duration of the current political upheaval, to escape into a frivolous world where true love is rewarded and people can make jokes.

Ayrshire Romantic

D. J. TAYLOR

The great wave of Romanticism that swept over Scottish literature from the mid-Victorian era onwards was always going to have its answering cry. This tendency was particularly marked among the group of twentieth-century writers who had grown up in its paralysing shadow. There you were, in your draughty schoolroom somewhere near Inverness, being lectured about Queen Victoria's 'Jacobite moods' and having it dinned into your head that *Waverley* was the greatest novel ever written north of the Tweed, while outside the window the unemployment queues grew longer and the winds swept in from continental Europe.

In these circumstances a work like Lewis Grassic Gibbon's *A Scots Quair* trilogy (1932–4), whose lyrical treatment of life in Kincardineshire is always undercut by a kind of bedrock realism, was a perfectly understandable reaction to what had gone before. But one curious aspect of the dozens of novels written in almost conscious opposition to Sir Walter Scott, kailyards and stickit ministers was how closely they began to resemble the thing they were rebelling against. And so Gordon Williams's *From Scenes Like These*, though set on the most dismal Ayrshire farmstead known to Scottish agriculture and featuring a fine old collection of toughs, seducers and misanthropes, soon reveals itself as a deeply romantic book.

Published in the autumn of 1968 and included on the following

---

Gordon Williams, *From Scenes Like These* (1968), appears in a compendium volume of four Scottish novels, *Growing up in the West* · Canongate · Pb · 744pp · £16 · ISBN 9781891952628.

year's inaugural Booker shortlist alongside Iris Murdoch and Muriel Spark, *Scenes* should ideally have propelled Gordon, or Gordon M., or G. M. Williams (the title-page rubric varies) firmly towards the summit of literature's Mount Olympus. As it was, he opted to follow its delicately ground-down realism with a pot-boiling thriller – *The Siege of Trencher's Farm* (1969) – written in the space of a fortnight.

This, it turns out, was entirely characteristic of Williams's no-nonsense approach to the business of making a living. Even by the standards of a literary generation that prided itself on its versatility, there is something altogether prodigious about the range of his out-put and the half-dozen professional worlds he inhabited: not many Grub Street irregulars could boast, as he was able to do in the half-decade between 1966 and 1971, of having had one novel shortlisted for the Booker and another filmed by Hollywood while carrying out ghost-writing assignments for an England football captain. (The football captain was Bobby Moore. The film director was Sam Peckinpah, who turned *The Siege of Trencher's Farm* into the voyeur-istic bloodbath that is *Straw Dogs*.)

On the other hand, the career that followed these early triumphs is so tantalizingly undocumented that you sometimes feel that what their author really needs is one of those 'in search of . . .' biographers, fixated and intrepid and willing to dedicate years of his or her life to the task of – say – tracking down some of the 28 separate addresses that Williams claimed to have lived at before the age of 23.

What is indisputably known about him is that he was a police-man's son from Paisley who broke into journalism in the early 1960s by way of a feature writer's job on the *Daily Mail*-sponsored *Weekend* magazine. By the end of the decade he was making huge amounts of money out of fiction (the film rights for his 1967 novel, *The Man Who Had Power over Women*, went to Paramount for £27,000 – about a quarter of a million pounds today). As for what happened in the 1980s when he veered off into screen-writing, beyond some mid-decade documentary work and a Channel 4 adaptation of Ruth

Rendell's *Tree of Hands* (1989), the trail soon winds away into desert.

If all Williams's novels are worth reading, then *From Scenes Like These* is his masterpiece: one of those raw, intensely felt books whose themes and preoccupations look as if they were chosen with the deliberate aim of parading the writer's gifts and with a prefatory paragraph that, rather like the quick-fire impressionism of Dickens's early work, instantly betrays its author's training as a journalist:

> It was still dark, that Monday in January, when the boy, Dunky Logan, and the man, Blackie McCann, came to feed and water the horses, quarter after seven on a cold Monday morning in January, damn near as chill as an Englishman's heart, said McCann, stamping his hobnail boots on the stable cobbles.

Craig's Farm, where these two unfortunates have fetched up – sometime in the mid-1950s to judge from the references to Eden, Macmillan and Attlee – is an environment in flux, its once rolling acres giving way to the expanding township nearby and a succession crisis looming as son and potential heir Willie schemes to succeed his ailing octogenarian father. While there are several different points of focus, including a sub-plot involving a newly arrived housekeeper pregnant by her last employer and scheming for a husband, most of the action revolves around Dunky and what Williams clearly regards as his principal subject: his teenage hero's wholesale corruption by the society of which he is a part.

Going on 16, living in the family home with his mother, sister and grim, bed-bound Logan senior, Dunky spends the majority of the book's 300 or so pages quietly turning from one kind of person into another. Almost before you can say 'Two pints of heavy and a couple of chasers' the vaguely well-meaning, rabbit-breeding, 'nice-girl' courting boy with ambitions to play professional football or emigrate to Canada has warped into a cynical drunk, of whose outlook his former schoolteacher remarks: 'I pity Logan and envy him at the same time. I know his life's being wasted, but he doesn't, he'll just sail along, sex, booze and football, thinking he's having a great time.' There is a rather awful scene, early on, in which Dunky recalls his individualistic grandfather, who registered as a conscientious objector during the Great War, and wonders 'Maybe he was a nutcase throwback . . . ? That wasn't a very cheery prospect, all he wanted to be was like everybody else.'

Yet for all the vigour of its attack on Scottish ideas of masculinity, and its attempt to locate within that behavioural template what the *Guardian* reviewer of 1968 called 'the springs of violence', *Scenes* is still an intensely romantic work, full of idealistic daydreaming, starry-eyed attempts to block out the realities that lie to hand or weld personal mythologizing on to a world of 'tattie-howking' (potato-picking) and back-breaking labour.

I first came across the London Library's battered hardback copy in the early 1990s. By the end of the decade, I was ready to track its author down. Curiously, older literary friends, so helpful if one wanted anecdotes about Philip Larkin or Kingsley Amis, could remember almost nothing about Gordon Williams. In fact, the only eyewitness I could turn up was Melvyn Bragg, who recalled an epic early 1970s pub crawl along the Thames, the night coming to a belated end at the Williams home in Notting Hill where both men were righteously bawled out by Williams's wife, Claerwen.

Interestingly, there are several references to Williams in *Venables* (1994), the autobiography of the former England football manager Terry Venables, with whom he collaborated on *They Used to Play on Grass* (1972) and the Hazell detective series, later televised, but these too tend to be face-down-in-the-vichysoisse moments. 'Gordon obviously had a bit of an alcohol problem,' Venables concludes at the end of a story in which his helpmate has come to blows with the sports journalist Hugh McIlvanney at Bobby Moore's testimonial dinner, 'but to his credit he went on to beat it and has not had a drink in a long time.'

Years passed. One millennium yielded to another, but still Williams remained out of reach, like some mysterious sybil obstinately concealing herself from the public gaze. There was no word of any future projects. And then, in 2003, after the censors had finally agreed to award a DVD certificate to *Straw Dogs*, came the news that Bloomsbury were reissuing *The Siege of Trencher's Farm* and that the author was willing to do a little publicity. We met in a Soho café not far from *Private Eye*'s offices in Carlisle Street with the aim of constructing a *Guardian* profile. Williams, then not far off 70, was affable but cagey. Although he claimed to be writing fiction again, and at one point presented me with a scrap of paper bearing wholly unintelligible lines from a work in progress, he would say nothing about the intervening twenty years. Intrigued but baffled, I soon beat a retreat.

Gordon Williams died in 2017 at the age of 83, leaving a set of obituaries high on praise but notably short on detail. Readers keen to know what kind of man he was, or imagined himself to be, are invited to grub for clues in what, for my money, is one of the finest Scottish novels of the twentieth century.

D. J. TAYLOR's books include *Orwell: The Life*, which won the 2003 Whitbread Biography Prize, and *The Prose Factory: Literary Life in England since 1918*. Of his dozen novels, the most recent is *Rock and Roll Is Life: The True Story of the Helium Kids by One Who Was There* (2018).

The Fanny Factor

LAURIE GRAHAM

It was some time in the mid-Sixties when things began to change in my mother's kitchen. First we got a fridge. Farewell mesh-doored meat safe, farewell flecks of curdled milk floating in your tea. The second thing that happened was Fanny Cradock.

This was a brief love affair – my mum later transferred her culinary trust and affection to Delia Smith – but while it lasted its impact was astonishing. Expenditure on piping bags, time spent tracking down a butter curler and a grapefruit knife, foods coloured contrary to the laws of Nature: the responsibility for this and much more could be laid at Fanny's door.

My mother was a typical post-war housewife, a thrifty provider of good, plain cooking. It's hard now to picture a time when every pantry contained packets of blancmange powder, when olive oil was something you bought at the chemist for use in cases of earache. But so it was. Our kitchen bible was a 1937 edition of *Cookery Illustrated & Household Management*. I have it still. It has recipes for Boiled Smelts and Cabinet Pudding, hints on the best season to buy capercailzie (September to November) and not one but *two* home remedies for lumbago.

In the Beginning was Philip Harben, but we didn't know about him. When Fanny burst upon the scene we had only just acquired a television, so my mum was an impressionable cookery-show virgin and Fanny Cradock swept her off her feet. Not only did Fanny cook

Fanny Cradock, *Coping with Christmas* (1968), is out of print, but we can try to obtain second-hand copies.

34

wearing lipstick and no apron, she was also a seductive blend of straight talking and aspirational glamour. Old enough to have weathered wartime rationing and prescient enough to recognize that the British public was ready for something new: tiddled-up food.

Where did she spring from, this born-for-television phenomenon? She'd been a travel journalist and a restaurant reviewer, presumably before her eyebrows and oak-smoked voice made her instantly recognizable. She was also a prodigious sausage machine of novels and, somewhat surprisingly, of children's books. Fanny's novels are what you might expect. The language tends towards the over-wrought and the groundwork was done by her research elves, possibly cousins of the kitchen elves who were always on hand to spirit away messy saucepans.

If you'd like a taster of Fanny's novels, I recommend *The Lormes of Castle Rising* (1975), the first of her grand country-house sagas, larded with lashings of below-stairs goings-on – all very Downton. And strangely, for a work of fiction, it has explanatory footnotes, in case you don't know your *Rognons en Brochette* from your *Mousseline de Soie*. It's as though Fanny, as a novelist, wasn't sure whether she wanted to be upstairs huntin', shootin' and eatin', or in the kitchen directing ops. For me, one of her most revealing television cookery tips was, 'Now, have this rushed through for service while it's piping hot.' It could be a line from one of her novels.

Where did it all come from? There was no Mrs Patmore in Fanny's childhood. Her parents flitted from hotel to hotel, one step ahead of debt collectors. But somewhere along the line she caught Escoffier Fever and with it that cruise-ship buffet tendency to over-adorn.

Her life story – her own version of which she gave in *Something's Burning* (1960) – was as bizarre as her appearance. She had four husbands, sometimes two at a time. To be a bigamist once may be regarded as a misfortune. To do it twice looks like carelessness. Fanny was a serial bolter and her children, whom she dumped on their grandparents, grew up not knowing her. When they met her, later in

© Getty Images

life, they didn't like her and the feeling was entirely mutual. In Fanny's heyday it was quite common for women to lie about their age, but she did it with the same bravura she brought to whipped cream piping. When she eventually married her fourth husband, Major Johnnie Cradock, she lopped off a jaw-dropping fifteen years for the official record, thereby making medical history by having given birth at the age of 5.

Many of Fanny's books and leaflets have disappeared from circulation, among them, to my very great regret, *Coping with Christmas* (1968). If you have a copy, treasure it.

'Coping', I think you'll agree, is not a neutral word. It suggests a hill to be climbed, a burden to be borne. Well, gimlet-eyed Fanny told it the way she saw it. 'Let us not delude ourselves,' she wrote, 'Christmas dinner is a monstrous intake of the world's most indigestible food.' The words 'sheer hell' and 'plague of relations' also crop up. Although not round at Fanny's, one imagines. She'd fallen out with all of them.

You could be forgiven for thinking that Fanny's heart just wasn't in the Christmas project, but she was a woman with a mission: to give her readers a blueprint for Christmas which left absolutely no eventuality uncatered for. I don't know about you, but fuse wire has never been on my Countdown to Christmas list, and neither has 'make dental appointment'. What a very far cry from Mary, who set out from Nazareth with nary a provision for the possibility that the days might be accomplished that she should be delivered.

But back to Fanny. 'Ideally,' she wrote, 'your preparations begin in

July, with preserved raspberries.' Not quite true. Elsewhere she exhorts us to make our puddings in January and then take them out of storage once a month to inspect them for mildew and give them a quick basting with brandy. My mum followed this palaver to the letter and her puddings were superb. Of the green brandy butter fashioned into a Christmas tree, perhaps the least said the better, but having invested in a butter curler I suppose she felt under pressure to use it.

Fanny also advised on how to deal with unexpected guests. In our house we did it by turning off the lights and sitting very still until they stopped knocking at the door and went away. Fanny, though, never missed an opportunity to demonstrate how completely sorted she was. Had we wished to emulate her we'd have made sure always to have a spare Swiss roll panel on standby for an impromptu *Bûche de Noël*. It might be one you'd made earlier, or one you whipped up effortlessly while your other half plied the unexpected guests with sherry. Either option invites the question, why bother?

Rolling up a Swiss roll without it cracking is *such* a test of nerves. Personally, I'd have thought a crack would lend a realistic touch, especially if you follow Fanny's instructions to slather the log in mocha buttercream and then rough it up bark-like with a cocktail stick. Besides, what kind of ungrateful chancers would quibble at a cracked *Bûche*?

As they achieved fame and fortune Fanny and Johnnie became quite grand. They got a Bentley and a place on the Côte d'Azur. Whether they awarded themselves a family crest, I don't know, but had they done so, a very fitting motto would have been 'Garnish and Present'.

Fanny could leave no lily ungilded and this tendency, picked up by my mum, was the cause of ructions between my usually devoted parents. My dad was a house painter. His working days were spent on building sites where men were men and their lunchtime grub was a sort of urban ploughman's: big sandwiches (crusts on) and perhaps a wedge of pork pie or fruit cake. Definitely not a pastry *barquette* filled with cream cheese and chopped celery and steered with a Twiglet rudder. Burly bricklayers and plumbers gathered around to witness my dad's unmanning. The verdict was that my mother had developed notions. At home that evening, words were exchanged. Then the United Nations were brought in and a compromise was reached. My mother was free to go Full Fanny in the privacy of her own home, but there was to be no more tiddling with Dad's lunchbox.

A signature Fanny touch was to make the edible look like the inedible. I'll let a veil fall over her Banana Candle, but I must mention her choux pastry swans and chestnut stuffing ducks swimming on a pond of green aspic. Even honest dishes like mashed potato got the treatment, dyed green and piped into Duchesse swirls. Fanny was a one-woman lobbyist for the glacé cherry and candied angelica industries. How have they fared since her demise, I wonder? Perhaps *Bake Off* has given them a fresh boost.

Mincemeat, homemade of course, was also a big item with Fanny. She was the touchpaper that ignited a mince pie revolution in our house. Normally the high priestess of fiddle and faff, she ordained that individual pies were a nuisance to make and a disappointment to eat: too much pastry, too little filling. The answer was a family-size pie, to be served in slices, and so it was in our house, ever after. Her big pie had merit. If only one could say the same for her Mincemeat Omelette. Don't. Just . . . don't.

But back to those Christmas preparations you should have made in the summer. Peach jam for the Boxing Day trifle? Tsk, tsk. What about new potatoes? Fanny's method was to take one of those deep merchant's biscuit tins and store freshly lifted baby potatoes between layers of sawdust. I think you then buried the tin in the garden until Christmas Eve. I'm sure it was all made clear in the booklet. But Fanny, isn't the joy of new potatoes that they mean summer has arrived? And doesn't everyone want crunchy roast potatoes on Christmas Day?

Christmas Cradock-style was much photographed, probably in

August, given magazine production schedules. The groaning board, the swags and garlands and royal-icing penguins, Fanny with a hair ribbon, Johnnie with his monocle. What were they really like after the curtain came down? Did they ever sit around in their jarmies, eating crisps? And what became of them when the TV circus moved on and their moment of celebrity passed?

They had no family. Johnnie had abandoned his own children when he met Fanny, and Fanny's two sons had long since voted with their feet. So there they were, the henpecked old buffer and the lemon-lipped termagant, saddled with each other for the duration. It wasn't a happy ending. Fanny didn't 'do' illness. She abandoned Johnnie as he lay dying and after his death she lived alone, descending into squalor and battiness until a few remaining friends rescued her.

Will the wheel of foodie fashion ever turn back to doing things Fanny-style? It's hard to imagine and yet she still has a following. Undecided how to stuff your turkey? Anxious lest your petits fours emerge from the oven blighted with inner goo? Get yourself over to YouTube where dear departed Fanny still has thousands of viewers. Piping bags at the ready!

LAURIE GRAHAM is the author of the often mis-shelved novel *Perfect Meringues* and has form as the inserter of dodgy recipes in her novels, *The Future Home-makers of America* and *The Early Birds*. She does not own a butter curler.

Anguish Revisited

POSY FALLOWFIELD

At boarding school in the late Sixties we had as our English teacher a Miss J. H. B. Jones. Coaxing us self-absorbed teenagers through the A-level syllabus she was diffident, patient and unassuming, and had it not been for a brief conversation in which she suggested I read *The Death of the Heart* (1938) by Elizabeth Bowen, I'm sorry to say I would by now have forgotten her utterly. But I went off for the long summer holiday and took her advice; I have my Penguin copy fifty years later, and the cover illustration of a young girl wearing an anguished expression still takes me back to those inevitably anguished years.

The novel is divided into three sections: 'The World', 'The Flesh' and 'The Devil'. In the first we discover Portia Quayne, a newly orphaned 16-year-old who has been taken in by her much older brother Thomas and his wife, Anna. This well-heeled couple live in some style on the edge of London's Regent's Park in a beautiful, immaculate house into which Portia, whose life has been spent shuffling between continental boarding-houses and shabby hotels, does not readily fit. There is a complicated back story, efficiently delivered in the first chapter, explaining how Portia's childhood was lived in an atmosphere of some disgrace and how Thomas and Anna, thoroughly respectable if not noticeably happy, have reluctantly accepted that they must do the right thing and give Portia a home.

They appear to be doing their best: she is given new clothes and a

Elizabeth Bowen, *The Death of the Heart* (1938)
Vintage · Pb · £9.99 · 368pp · ISBN 9780099276456

pretty room, sent to private lessons, allowed a certain amount of freedom. But Anna has found – and read – Portia's diary and it has rattled her (although we are told little about what Portia has actually written, apart from the fact that 'there does not seem to be a single thing that she misses'). Anna's already brittle self-esteem feels under threat and she angrily tells a friend that Portia has 'made nothing but trouble since before she was born'.

Portia, meanwhile, yearning for some sign of affection from her brother, is trying to fit in; her greatest ally is Matchett, an elderly housemaid who has been inherited from Thomas's mother along with the furniture. This family retainer, who knew and respected Portia's father, comforts the child by talking to her about him; they have secret whispered conversations after Portia is in bed in which Matchett, generally so tight-lipped, tries to give her a proper sense of her value within the family. She is the one person, we feel, who properly cares about the child, watching her comings and goings, noticing her chilblains, worrying about her absent-mindedness.

Unfortunately, Portia – not yet old enough to be discerning, and badly in need of affection – has her head turned by Eddie, one of Anna's sillier friends. Major Brutt, on the other hand, a past acquaintance of Anna's encountered by chance, proves a real friend. He starts to call on the Quaynes, often uninvited, charmed by Portia and – ironically – by what he perceives to be the happy family atmosphere of the house.

The second section, 'The Flesh', in which Portia is introduced to a set of young people all boisterously asserting themselves, contains some sublime comedy. Anna and Thomas have, a little guiltily, escaped to Capri for a holiday and Portia is sent to stay with Mrs Heccomb, Anna's one-time governess who now lives in a house by the sea with her stepchildren, who are exquisitely drawn. Daphne and Dickie are loud, bossy, serenely self-confident and seem to Portia 'a crisis that surely must be unique: she could not believe that they happened every day'. Daphne works in a library:

Portia realized later that the tomb-like hush of Smoot's library, where she had to sit all day, dealing out hated books, was not only antipathetic but even dangerous to Daphne. So, once home, she kept fit by making a loud noise. Daphne never simply touched objects, she slapped down her hand on them; she made up her mouth with the gesture of someone cutting their throat.

The seaside house, Waikiki, noisy with creaks and bangs and loud music, could hardly be more different from the Quaynes' London house. At 2 Windsor Terrace, Thomas telephones Anna from his study to report he is home, silently brooding downstairs while she entertains above; Portia lets herself in quietly and creeps about, anxious not to disturb. At Waikiki, however, everyone knows what everyone else is doing – partly because of the acoustics, but also because there seems to be nothing to hide.

Portia is beginning to enjoy herself here when Eddie turns up, at her invitation; Mrs Heccomb, who had been expecting a respectable friend of Anna's, is taken aback by his 'bounce'. 'Each time he spoke, her eyes went to his forehead, to the point where his hair sprang back in its fine spirited waves . . . Portia could almost hear Mrs Heccomb's ideas, like chairs before a party, being rolled about and rapidly rearranged.'

The young people all go to the cinema and Portia's world crashes about her ears when she sees Eddie holding Daphne's willing hand. She tackles him about this and Eddie, who is incapable of considering anyone else, is perhaps not shocked enough by the evident strength of Portia's feeling for him. After his return to London, however, the rest of Portia's stay passes tranquilly: everybody is kind, and when she leaves, her diary entry is forlorn:

> I cannot say anything about going away . . . Perhaps it is better not to say anything ever. I must try not to say anything more to Eddie, when I have said things it has always been a mistake.

The final section, 'The Devil', is where the real anguish comes in. Portia, adrift and unhappy, becomes desperate when she learns that Anna has read her diary. Convinced that Eddie and Anna have been laughing at her, she confronts Eddie who, as ever, slithers away from a direct question. Feeling she has nothing to lose, Portia now takes a bold step and frightens Thomas and Anna – she throws down a challenge to them and waits to see how they will respond. It's an anguished wait, for the reader too.

Elizabeth Bowen builds her characters through superbly written conversations, provides history and context, gives everyone a hinterland. (They also, most definitely, have a future.) The vain, the shallow, the thoughtless, all behave as they do for a reason. Anna, who can be cruel, has herself suffered cruelties – a jilting lover, two miscarriages – and, further, has no illusions about herself. Thomas, outwardly successful, is miserable: 'We none of us seem to feel very well, and I don't think we want each other to know it.' But this is not a bleak book; understanding dawns at the end.

Angus McBean photograph (MS Thr 581),
© Houghton Library, Harvard University

Among the joys of the novel are the thumbnail sketches. Mrs Heccomb, responsible for Portia, worries about the letters she is getting: 'She looked pink. On top of this she wore, like an extra hat, a distinct air of caution and indecision. "It is so nice to get letters," she said.'

Major Brutt, so doggedly trying to land a job, is tragically summed up: 'Makes of men date, like makes of cars; Major Brutt was a 1914–18 model; there was now no market for that make.' And the incomparable Matchett, whose 'step on the parquet or on the staircase was at the same time ominous and discreet', is described elsewhere as 'the woman with the big stony apron, who backs to the wall when I pass like a caryatid'.

It is not only the characters who provide both tragedy and comedy; the places do too. There is a moving description of Portia's rootless childhood, remembered with longing:

> They always stayed in places before the season, when the funicular was not working yet. All the other people in that pension had been German or Swiss: it was a wooden building with fretwork balconies. Their room, though it was a back room facing into the pinewoods, had a balcony; they would run away from the salon and spend the long wet afternoons there. They would lie down covered with coats, leaving the window open, smelling the wet woodwork, hearing the gutters run . . .

The interior of 2 Windsor Terrace is, despite its comforts, home to considerable unhappiness:

> The vibration of London was heard through the shuttered and muffled window as though one were half deaf; lamplight bound the room in rather unreal circles; the fire threw its hard glow on the rug. The house held such tense, positive quiet that he and she might have been all alone in it.

Waikiki is (literally) a breath of fresh air:

> While she was up in her room combing her hair back, hearing the tissue paper in her suitcase rustle, watching draughts bulge the new matting strip, she heard the bang that meant Daphne was in. Waikiki was a sounding box . . . In her room, the electric light, from its porcelain shade, poured down with a frankness unknown at Windsor Terrace. The light swayed slightly in that seaside draught, and Portia felt a new life had begun.

Perhaps most powerful of all, though, is the description of the Karachi Hotel in South Kensington where Major Brutt is staying:

> The public rooms are lofty and large . . . nothing so nobly positive as space. The fireplaces with their flights of brackets, the doors with their poor mouldings, the nude-looking windows exist in deserts of wall: after dark the high-up electric lights die high in the air above unsmiling armchairs. If these houses give little by becoming hotels, they lose little . . . Their builders must have built to enclose fog, which having seeped in never quite goes away. Dyspepsia, uneasy wishes, ostentation, and chilblains can, only, have governed the lives of families here.

Of course, anyone might have suggested reading Elizabeth Bowen, and anyone might have recommended starting with *The Death of the Heart*, but it was Miss Jones who did so and it is to Miss Jones that I am forever grateful. If we at the time felt anything for our English teacher it would have been that unattractive condescending pity bestowed by adolescents on middle-aged teachers and, with the callousness of youth, I never thought to write and thank her. Subsequently, and too late, I regretted this, but I realize now my pity was misplaced; if she was familiar with Elizabeth Bowen then her life can't have been as empty as all that.

POSY FALLOWFIELD – having had a stab at teaching herself – has a healthy respect for teachers these days, feeling that good ones are worth their weight in gold.

Love and Friendship

MAGGIE FERGUSSON

Back in the 1990s, when I began to work for the Royal Society of Literature, I suddenly found myself surrounded by writers I'd admired for years, but never dreamt I'd meet – Sybille Bedford, John Mortimer, Hilary Mantel, Victoria Glendinning, Penelope Fitzgerald. I can't remember the exact occasion on which I was first introduced to Rose Tremain, but I do remember feeling a little apprehensive. Not only was she a novelist whose work I loved, she was also very beautiful. I needn't have worried. She was, from the start, friendly, natural, wickedly good-humoured and warm – such good company, in fact, that I was, at first, a little disappointed that she wanted to conduct this interview by email. Then I realized that this was an act of generosity. 'It's much more possible for me to get really interesting ideas and explorations going,' she explained, 'if I can write them down.'

*

One summer's evening, at the age of 13 or 14, Rose Tremain had what she describes as 'an epiphany'. She had been playing tennis with friends at school, but was alone, when she was overcome with the certainty that writing was 'the only thing I wanted to do'; that her life would be half-lived if not devoted to words.

It would be quite a while before she was able to live out this conviction – when her first novel was published she was in her early thirties – but in the fullness of time Rose Tremain was to become one

Rose Tremain, *Restoration* (1989), *Merivel: A Man of His Time* (2012), *The Gustav Sonata* (2016) and *Rosie* (2018) are all available as Vintage paperbacks from £8.99 each.

of the most prolific and best-loved novelists of her generation, winner of a host of prizes, including the Orange, the Whitbread and the James Tait Black. 'She's a true stylist,' Ian McEwan says of her. 'A writer who cares about her novels at the level of the sentence.'

Her subjects are sometimes contemporary, even prescient. In *Sacred Country* (1992) she explored, well ahead of its time, transgender life, while in *The Road Home* (2007) she considered the economic lot of the migrant. But she is perhaps best known as a historical novelist. The historian Niall Ferguson has said that historical fiction 'contaminates historical understanding'. What is her response to this? Ferguson can be right, she replies. Historical fiction that reimagines the lives of real characters gives her what she calls 'biographical unease' – 'you keep wanting to say, "Is this true or isn't it?", and rush back to the history books'. So, if real historical figures are to play parts in her novels, she insists that they are seen 'ONLY through the eyes of the invented people'.

Perhaps the invented character who has most haunted Rose Tremain, and her readers, is Robert Merivel, a courtier to King Charles II, a joyful, wanton, blundering, yearning man constantly thrown back by the king's displeasure on his friendship with an austere Quaker doctor, John Pearce. Merivel is impossible not to love, making us laugh over one page and weep over the next. When she first introduced him in *Restoration* (1989) her aim was to reflect the climate of materialism and excess under Margaret Thatcher. She was searching for 'a mirror age' in which similar radical change came very fast. The return of Charles II in 1660, 'bringing colour and noise and selfish, showy abandon back into a society so long clad in puritan black', seemed the perfect historical moment.

From the first page of the novel readers have a powerful sense of being immersed in the mid-seventeenth century; yet whatever research has gone into it is lightly worn. 'Research should never show up as data,' says Rose. 'It should just be quietly there, behind the scenes, giving the reader confidence that the author knows the territory.

Rose Tremain wrote *Restoration* at a difficult time in her life, when she was 'in a fragile emotional state', about to go through a bitter divorce. She cried a lot while she worked on it. But she thinks, looking back, that 'feeling vulnerable and frightened was perfect for this piece of work, which explores human frailty and folly. Merivel's life is always poised on the cliff edge of disaster, as mine was poised on the precipice of separation and change.' As a reader, I felt bereft at turning the last page of this romp-cum-tragedy, and Rose 'missed him like mad' when she finished the novel – though it wasn't until years later that she decided to return to him in *Merivel: A Man of His Time* (2012).

Romantic love is a magnet for novelists. But Rose is at least equally fascinated by 'love's quieter relation – friendship'. Friendship, she has written, 'is a formative and precious thing, able to influence our moral positioning in the world, teach us the rules of kindness and generosity, and anchor us to sanity when times are bad'. In *The Gustav Sonata* (2016) she traces an intense and often painful friendship between two men, Gustav Perle and Anton Zwiebel, that lasts for sixty years, beginning when they meet at primary school in Switzerland, just after the end of the Second World War. The Switzerland the boys grow up in is not one filled with the 'plainchant of cowbells', but a dull place where Gustav's mother, Emilie, works in a cheese factory. A penurious widow, Emilie treats Gustav cruelly, slapping his knuckles with a ruler, squashing his hopes and desires. But Gustav's love for Anton – a gifted, highly strung musician – is unshakable. On holiday near Davos, the boys find a derelict sanatorium, and among the ghosts of the dead play at doctor and patient. An innocent game mingles with stirrings of adolescence and they exchange a lingering kiss. It's the most powerful moment in the book, and the most 'strangely beautiful' in Gustav's life.

Rose has compared *The Gustav Sonata* to a Swiss watch. The novel is deceptively easy to read, 'just as the faces of Swiss watches are clear and easy to read. They appear to do a very simple job, which in fact is not simple at all, but the product of sophisticated knowledge and engineering work.' The language is simple and unadorned, while the story being told is actually very carefully and minutely assembled.

Like Merivel, though in a very different way, Gustav is a character easy to love. Given how much he suffers, I wonder how it was possible to make him so sympathetic without sentimentalizing him? 'The core thing about Gustav is that he never indulges in self-pity. Thus, the reader is free to pity him as much or as little as he/she feels inclined to, but he never sentimentalizes his sufferings, never specifically cajoles the reader into feeling sorry for him. Even as a man, when Anton goes away to Geneva and all seems lost, Gustav just gets on with his day-to-day life. In the end, I think this is what moves us – his famous "self-mastery".'

Much of Gustav's suffering has its roots in his troubled relationship with his mother, and I wonder whether Emilie Perle has similarities to Rose's own mother, Jane? Yes and no. Jane, Rose says, 'was a snob and self-deluding and Emilie Perle is neither of these'. But Emilie does know, as Rose's mother did, how to put her child down. Even when Gustav has some success in setting up and running a hotel, Emilie can't appreciate what he's done or praise him, and this was very much Rose's experience with her mother. She died in 2001, but nothing Rose had achieved as a writer up to that time, including a Booker shortlisting, 'was ever considered worthy of any serious attention by Jane Thomson'.

Rose has written that 'knowledge is a powerful thing, and knowing when to keep it secret is an art which every serious writer needs to perfect'. Perhaps it's not surprising, then, that it's only relatively recently – and prompted by a conversation with her daughter, Eleanor – that she has chosen to share the story of her childhood in a memoir, *Rosie* (2018). It makes for much unhappy, and even sometimes shocking, reading. While Rose and her sister, Jo, lacked for nothing materially – in one memorable scene she describes her grandparents' butler serving them lemonade from a silver salver in their tree-house – they were neglected, and then abandoned, by their father, and treated by their mother with a cool indifference that sometimes shaded into cruelty.

Reproduced in *Rosie* is a glowing school report, in which the head-mistress writes that Rose is 'an exceptionally gifted girl'. The only less-than-perfect note is struck by the gym mistress, who says she needs to work harder. 'Ha! Ha!' her mother has scrawled next to this. But for the unwavering love of her nanny, Vera Sturt, to whom the book is dedicated, Rose might have been emotionally crippled for life.

In periods of suffering, she has always found solace in writing fiction. But writing a memoir was different. 'While I've always been able to keep a fruitful distance between myself and my invented char-acters, in order to see them honestly and clearly and to ward off sentimentality, the distance between Rose and "Rosie" was not wider than the chambers of my heart. In order to write about Rosie I had to *recover* Rosie deep inside myself and make her breathe again.'

Rose had hoped that writing about her 'loveless parents' might enable her to forgive them, but this did not happen: she felt no for-giveness at all. 'The deeper I went into an evocation of the past, the more I realized how little they had ever understood me or tried to help me towards a fruitful life.'

How amazed her mother would have been – and how irked – if she'd known just how fruitful Rose's life would be. Quite apart from her success as a writer, she is happily married to Richard Holmes, one of the great biographers of all time, and is a doting grandmother. Just as you can make decisions to change your external landscape, she believes, you can make decisions to change your internal landscape too. But is there any danger that contentment might make her writ-ing bland – that happiness might begin to 'write white'? Not at all, she insists. 'Joyful moments full of laughter can engage all one's writ-erly energy and be very powerful on the page.'

MAGGIE FERGUSSON is Literary Editor of *The Tablet*, and is looking forward to a new novel by Rose Tremain next year.

Have I Already Told You . . . ?

OLIVER PRITCHETT

Two common afflictions of old age – apart from creaky knees – are acute reminiscence and chronic anecdote. I suffer from both. As I get older I forget how many times I have told the same story to the same friends, and they, luckily, have forgotten how many times they have heard it before. I suppose this must be the special charm of gentlemen's clubs: old men contentedly telling each other the same old tales.

Obviously, the telling of anecdotes can become a dangerous addiction; there's the risk of becoming like the chap who has memorized a thousand jokes and relentlessly reels them off in the saloon bar. *The Oxford Book of Literary Anecdotes*, edited by the late James Sutherland and first published in 1975, is an honourable exception. I actually didn't realize I owned this volume until I discovered it by chance in my bookshelf a few months ago. Perhaps it crept into my house one night and insinuated itself between the Chambers *Dictionary of Literary Characters* and *Who's Who in Shakespeare's England*. (There's a good story behind that.)

Professor Sutherland's collection (not to be confused with *The New Oxford Dictionary of Literary Anecdotes,* published in 2006, which has yet to invade my shelves) is never a bore. Even the subject index is a delight, covering such topics as Tactlessness, Sin, the usefulness of, Banalities, Disillusionment and Disinterment. You can see at once that this is the perfect book for dipping into, and if you feel that

---

James Sutherland (ed.), *The Oxford Book of Literary Anecdotes* (1975), is out of print, but we can obtain second-hand copies.

'dipping in' is not quite a respectable activity, Professor Sutherland has the answer for you.

This, he writes, is a book 'designed primarily for desultory reading'. Nobody, surely, can object to being considered a desultory reader. And the *Oxford Book* is full of desultory delights. It is arranged chronologically according to the literary figure who features in the anecdote, beginning with Caedmon, the Anglo-Saxon poet, and ending with Dylan Thomas. And there are extensive notes, giving the sources for everything.

Before discovering Professor Sutherland's collection, my favourite literary anecdote was a spoof, composed by Walter de la Mare, which is brilliantly inconsequential.

> My aged friend, Miss Wilkinson,
> Whose mother was a Lambe,
> Saw Wordsworth once, and Coleridge, too,
> One morning in her pram.
>
> Birdlike the bards stooped over her –
> Like fledgling in a nest;
> And Wordsworth said, 'Thou harmless babe!'
> And Coleridge was impressed.
>
> The pretty thing gazed up and smiled,
> And softly murmured 'Coo!'
> William was then aged sixty-four
> And Samuel sixty-two.

In some collections of anecdotes it seems that almost every one ends with a noted wit making some dazzlingly clever remark. You suspect that these tales are like pieces of family silver, taken out from time to time, primped and given a good polish. They can also be suspiciously pithy. Professor Sutherland's stories move at a more leisurely pace. They are mined from hundreds of (often half-forgotten) memoirs, biographies and letters, many of them about quite minor figures in literature, but all of them revealing in some way, even touching.

There is a delicious tale of the feud between the Irish writer George Moore and the three sisters who were his neighbours in Upper Ely Place, Dublin. It seems the ladies disapproved of his painting his front door green when all the others were white. (This has the flavour of a rather modern sort of neighbourly dispute.) They then bought a copy of his novel *Esther Waters*, tore it into small pieces, put them in an envelope, wrote 'Too filthy to keep in the house' on it and pushed it through his letterbox. Moore responded by making a habit of going out at eleven, twelve and one at night to rattle his stick along the Upper Ely Place railings in order to make the sisters' dog bark. They retaliated by hiring an organ grinder to play under his window while he was writing.

(Sorry to interrupt, but have I ever told you about the time I went on a chauffeur-driven pub crawl with Kingsley Amis? Five times? Really? As many as that?)

The desultory reader will surely enjoy the image of Robert Burton, author of *The Anatomy of Melancholy*, standing by a bridge in Oxford, holding his sides and laughing 'most profusely' as he listened to the bargemen raging and swearing at one another. This seems to have been his only pleasure. In his college rooms he was said to be 'so mute and mopish' that he was suspected of being suicidal.

A boatman also features in Lord Macaulay's diary of a trip to Ireland in 1849. Four rowers were sent to meet his party when they reached the head of Upper Lake in Killarney. One of the four was particularly proud of having rowed Sir Walter Scott and the Irish writer Maria Edgeworth twenty-four years previously. It was, he said, compensation for missing a hanging which had taken place on the same day.

(Talking of boat trips, remind me to tell you about the time I was visiting Guyana and, on an outing in a dug-out canoe in some remote part of the country, the boat overturned and I was forced to swim to the nearest bank of the river, where I discovered I was paying an unplanned visit to Venezuela.)

I have to admit, however, that my arrival in Venezuela was less dramatic and emotional than scenes that took place in New York in 1841, when waiting crowds of Dickens fans, desperate to know the fate of the heroine of *The Old Curiosity Shop*, which first appeared in instalments, stormed the piers, calling out to approaching ships 'Is Little Nell dead?' Thomas Carlyle was utterly overcome by the death of Little Nell, while Daniel O'Connell, the Irish MP, reading *The Old Curiosity Shop* on a train, was reported to have burst into tears and thrown the book out of the carriage window.

In the course of desultory reading I found this charming story about the eighteenth-century Scottish journalist and poet Thomas Campbell. At a literary dinner party, he proposed a toast to Napoleon Bonaparte. As hostilities with France were then at their height, this did not go down well with the rest of the company and Campbell's speech was nearly drowned out by the groans that greeted his words. He soldiered on:

> Gentlemen, you must not mistake me. I admit that the French Emperor is a tyrant. I admit that he is a monster. I admit that he is a sworn foe of our nation, and, if you will, of the whole human race. But, gentlemen, we must be just to our great enemy. We must not forget that he once shot a bookseller.

This was, of course, warmly applauded by all the literary guests. (Professor Sutherland's notes helpfully add that the bookseller – i.e. publisher – was the anti-French agitator Johann Philipp Palm of Nuremberg.)

Mention of parties, and the fact that Thomas Campbell was also a journalist, tempts me to tell you about the time I moved from my job at the *Guardian* and the guest of honour at my leaving party was Christine Keeler. But I will resist the temptation this time because I

Thomas Rowlandson, 'Bookseller and Author', watercolour

have just remembered an anecdote about Dylan Thomas, told by the novelist and BBC radio producer Rayner Heppenstall in his memoirs, and included in *The Oxford Book of Literary Anecdotes*. On a visit to Cornwall, Dylan and Caitlin Thomas and Rayner Heppenstall were going for a walk near Newlyn and, as they went along, Dylan was taking swigs from a flagon of some Penzance herbalist's highly intoxicating concoction called 'champagne wine tonic'.

Heppenstall recalls that Thomas was talking 'copiously'. Then suddenly he stopped. 'Somebody's boring me,' he said. 'I think it's me.'

The cue to end this piece.

OLIVER PRITCHETT must, at all costs, be dissuaded from writing his memoirs, after sixty years in journalism.

Airborne Division

MARTIN SORRELL

Of all Richard Wagner's music dramas, the one I know best is *Tristan und Isolde*, as do a lot of people, I imagine. I first came to it as an undergraduate, courtesy of the LPs lent me by my tutorial partner. At the age of 19, Henry was already an authority on Wagner, thanks in large part to the volunteer work he'd been doing for three years as a scene-shifter and odd-jobber at the Bayreuth Festival.

So it was that on the Dansette record player I'd brought from home, Kirsten Flagstad's Isolde, Ludwig Suthaus's Tristan and Josef Greindl's King Mark opened a window one misty afternoon on Wagner's dark, mythical world. I followed the triangular tragedy of illicit love until, some four hours later, it played out its doomed endgame in sumptuous chords and soaring melody. From time to time that winter, I'd borrow Henry's records again, not to hear the whole of *Tristan*, but just the two sections that wouldn't stop ringing in my head – the prelude to the third act, with its heartbreaking air for cor anglais, and, in the second act, the lament of the wronged King Mark.

That king, that love triangle, came back to me recently when I decided at last to read something by a French writer of whom I'd long since heard but had never had quite enough curiosity to investigate – Joseph Kessel. I'd paired him in my mind with another French novelist, equally 'minor', Maurice Dekobra. Born within a dozen years or so of each other, they were said to evoke better than most novelists of the time the glittering, bohemian-round-the-edges soci-

Joseph Kessel, *The Crew* (1923) · Trans. André Naffis-Sahely
Pushkin Press · Pb · 288pp · £12 · ISBN 9781782271611

ety of the twenty years between the two World Wars. Their names conjured up sybarites moving around the fleshpots of Europe in Lagondas and luxury trains and private aeroplanes, the Jay Gatsbys of an older continent.

Dekobra worked on my imagination for one detail in particular, the marvellously suggestive title of one of his novels, *The Madonna of the Sleeping Cars*. Kessel too could come up with strong titles – *The Army of Shadows*, for example. However, what he's remembered for above all is *Belle de Jour*, though I suspect that not everyone who's seen Buñuel's celebrated film knows that its origins lie in a fairly short book of Kessel's, published in 1928, no raunchy autobiography of a progressive and liberated woman but a rather average piece of fiction created by a thoroughly masculine man.

The Crew (*L'Equipage*), Kessel's semi-autobiographical novel of 1923, is a different proposition, if equally male. Elements of the Tristan and Isolde myth appear in the context of the First World War; more precisely, of a French aerial reconnaissance unit stationed close to the Western Front. What plays out over the course of twelve chapters is in effect a twentieth-century romance of chivalry that goes wrong. For medieval mounted charges, substitute aeroplanes locked in a dogfight. For shields and lances, substitute metal plating and machine guns. Instead of heroic verse, savour limpid, driving prose. And replace the aristocratic Belle Dame worshipped from a hygienic distance with a young Parisian wife far more eager to fall into her secret lover's arms than the marital bed.

The story, then – with a partial but necessary spoiler alert: 20-year-old Jean Herbillon leaves his family with a fairly light heart, and his mistress Denise with a still lighter one, to travel from Paris to the airfield in eastern France where the squadron he's joining is based. Once installed, he's quickly integrated into the brotherhood of flyers and ground staff who, between high-risk missions, josh and joke and drink and fool about in a pungently male environment that could be transposed to the RAF in Kent or Lincolnshire without the need to change anything other than a few names. The squadron's leader, Captain Gabriel Thélis, is a commanding presence, fearless, authoritative, calm under pressure, and revered by his men – an improbable catalogue of qualities in a young man of just 24. But if Thélis sounds an unlikely character, he does serve to remind us that so many airmen who fought and died in the two World Wars were barely more than lads fresh out of school.

The reconnaissance teams, the *équipages* described by Kessel, consist of a pilot and, seated behind him, an observer, the role played by Jean. Each team takes to the air armed with a machine gun and a camera, and typically flies over the battle zone and the enemy dispositions and, as often as not, limps back to base – the price of an encounter with German fighter planes that has left the pilot barely able to get the plane on the ground before the injured crewman, he or the observer is hauled out, only to expire from their injuries on the grass. Kessel does these set pieces without mawkishness or over-dramatization. On the contrary, he deploys enviable gifts of clarity and economy. And he has the sure touch of someone who knows precisely what aerial combat is about, for he himself had served in the French Air Force during the First World War.

Dead pilots have to be replaced, of course, and a few chapters into the novel it's one of the new arrivals, Claude Maury, who unwittingly gives the remainder of the story its Wagnerian overtones. Maury is a loner, quiet, thoughtful, troubled. He doesn't bond easily with the other men, but there is a natural affinity between him and the younger Jean, which deepens once the pair has become an established crew. A large part of Maury's trouble, which he confides to Jean, is that the deep and unswerving love he has for his wife Hélène is no longer reciprocated, at least not physically. When Jean goes back to Paris on leave, Maury asks him to deliver in person the letter he's written to Hélène. First, though, Jean has a passionate, but ominously troubled, reunion with Denise, and it's only later that he remembers Maury's letter. He makes his way to the address he's been given, is ushered in, and – here's the spoiler – comes face to face with . . . Denise. Hélène and Denise are one and the same woman.

Jean's mission to reconcile Hélène with Maury has gone awry, as irreversibly as Tristan's to bring Isolde across the sea from Ireland to marry King Mark. And from the moment Jean rejoins his unit to the novel's final chapter, the tone of the story becomes sombre. Jean tries to keep the greatest distance he can between himself and Maury, but the air sorties have to go on. So Maury and Jean continue as a crew, still united in its purpose but divided now by the guilt of one man and the suspicions of the other. Delicately, allusively, Kessel has the reader understand that Maury knows some kind of betrayal must have occurred, and that he has a hunch what kind it was.

To make matters worse, midway through the second part, the squadron's charismatic King Arthur figure, Gabriel Thélis, is killed. It's a loss that plunges his court of flyers, mechanics, observers and gunners into gloom; a cloud settles on their Camelot. Nonetheless, life and the war continue. Maury and Jean take to the air again, the cockpit of their plane a stifling enclosure of ever-mounting tension, until, in the last few pages, the situation is resolved, though not quite in the way I was expecting.

Since beginning to write this, I've reread *The Crew*, and I've found it even more powerful and elegantly constructed than I had the first time. It's no longer only the descriptions of aerial combat that strike me, nor just the Tristan and Isolde theme played out so poignantly. It's Kessel's skill in blending these two strands, ancient and modern, into a whole that's as sophisticated as it appears simple, as broad as it seems narrowly focused. *The Crew*, I realize, is an expert demonstration of the art of hiding art. And, second time round, I recognize this little novel as a masterpiece, a minor one maybe, but still a masterpiece.

MARTIN SORRELL now intends to have a second stab at the prolific Maurice Dekobra, many of whose titles sound just as inviting as *The Madonna of the Sleeping Cars*.

A Delight in Digression

DAVID SPILLER

In the north London suburb of Edmonton where I grew up, virtually the only feature of note is Charles Lamb's cottage in Church Street, which is marked with a blue plaque. The essayist lived there in the first half of the nineteenth century. Lamb was born in 1775 and in 1792 began thirty-three years of tedious work as a clerk at the East India Company counting-house. Over the length of his adult life he lived – on and off – with his sister Mary. Their story is told in Sarah Burton's highly readable *A Double Life: A Biography of Charles and Mary Lamb* (2003).

The incident that was to define the lives of both siblings occurred in 1796. Mary had a congenital mental condition, and in a fit of madness stabbed her mother through the heart while the family was at dinner. She was committed to a madhouse but within two and a half years was freed from official constraint and put into the care of her brother Charles. Yet in most years thereafter she needed to spend further time in care. A friend reported chancing upon the pair in

Charles Lamb's cottage on Church Street

Charles Lamb, *Essays of Elia* (1823), is available in various print-on-demand paperback editions. We can also obtain nice second-hand copies of earlier hardback editions.

the street one day as Charles, carrying a straitjacket, escorted his sister to Hoxton asylum.

The wretchedness of such scenes was in marked contrast to Mary's behaviour when in normal health. Their friend William Hazlitt wrote of 'the sweetness of her disposition, the clearness of her understanding, and the gentle wisdom of all her acts and words', and he seemed to speak for all who knew her. Charles was devoted to his sister and she to him. Their mutual supportiveness, in life and in their literary work, is often compared to that of Wordsworth and his sister Dorothy.

When Mary was well, the Lambs were renowned for their hospitality and – in Charles's case – a good deal of hard drinking. Friends included literary luminaries such as Coleridge, Wordsworth and Hazlitt, plus an unusually wide circle of eccentrics. Lamb wrote that he had never made any lasting friends 'that had not some tincture of the absurd in their characters'. His intimates 'were in the world's eye a ragged regiment. [I] found them floating on the surface of society.'

Against their extraordinary background it is surprising that the Lambs got any writing done at all. An early collaboration was their *Tales from Shakespeare* (1807), which summarized for children the plots of twenty plays and became the most successful thing either of them wrote – it is still in print today in more than a dozen editions. It was Mary who received the commission to write the *Tales* and did most of the work, though this has not always been made clear – witness the ascription of authorship on the title pages of modern editions, where Charles's name is always placed before his sister's, if indeed she gets mentioned at all. In fact the limpid clarity of the prose points to Mary, because her brother's writing was characterized by (in his own words) 'antique modes and phrases'.

Charles was slow to find the literary voice that ultimately made him famous. He started by contributing jokey anecdotes to the *Morning Post*, then had poems included in a collection edited by Coleridge and wrote some unsuccessful plays and some well-received literary criticism. From the age of 35 he began writing essays, and ten years later was contributing regularly to the *London Magazine*, which led eventually to a separate publication, *Essays of Elia* (1823). The pseudonym was borrowed from a clerk at South Sea House where Lamb had once worked. Elia was an anagram for 'a lie', which suited Lamb's custom of writing ironically under the guise of different voices, so that the reader never knew exactly who had done what. The medium was to bring Lamb a national reputation and to swell the always modest income that he and Mary survived on. It helped that this was the heyday of the essay form, with Lamb and Hazlitt its best-known practitioners.

In writing this article I used an edition of *Essays of Elia* that I'd hung on to as a keepsake. It came from a series of several dozen classic books that had belonged to my mother, and formed the bedrock of her intensive reading when – as the custom went in those days – she was sent out to work at the age of 15. She bought the books on subscription from Odham's Press during the 1920s and 1930s. They were identically bound in maroon with old-fashioned gold lettering on the spines.

It is hard to sum up the flavour of Lamb's essays. He had little interest in politics. The arts were well represented, with literature and the theatre prominent, but not music ('Organically I am incapable of a tune'). The unpredictability of subject matter is suggested by three essays that appear side by side: 'The Tombs in the Abbey' is a diatribe against the practice of charging for entrance to Westminster Abbey; 'Amicus redivivus' describes how a short-sighted friend of the family had to be rescued from drowning when he accidentally walked into the river near Lamb's house; and 'Barbara S—' records how a child actress, working thirty years before Lamb's birth, was mistakenly paid double the going rate for a week's work and agonized over whether to give the money back.

Nor is the title of an essay a reliable guide to its content, since Lamb was famous for his digressions. So 'The Old Margate Hoy' dwells briefly on the delights of a seaside holiday but is mostly about a fellow-passenger met on a boat who was 'the greatest liar I had met with then or since'; and 'Old China' has one page on Lamb's liking for china jars and saucers and four charming pages on how buying things gave Mary and himself the most pleasure in the days when they were poor.

Some essays manage to stay within the bounds of their nominal subject. 'A Dissertation upon a Roast Pig' floats the absurd conceit that roast pork was discovered when a Chinese family accidentally burnt down their flimsy cottage with a litter of newborn piglets inside. Raking through the remains, the father picked up an incinerated piglet and instinctively licked his fingers after burning them on the crackling. Thereafter neighbours noticed that every time the family's sow farrowed, the rebuilt cottage would be in flames again.

Perhaps the most affecting writing uses Lamb's idiosyncratic humour to illuminate unchanging elements of everyday life. 'Poor Relations', for instance:

> A poor relation is the most irrelevant thing in nature – a piece of impertinent correspondency – an odious approximation – a haunting conscience – a preposterous shadow, lengthening in the noon-tide of our prosperity . . . He is known by his knock . . .
>
> He entereth smiling and embarrassed . . . He casually looketh in about dinner time when the table is full. He offereth to go away, seeing you have company, but is induced to stay. He filleth a chair and your visitor's two children are accommodated at a side-table . . . He declareth against fish, the turbot being small, yet suffereth himself to be importuned into a slice, against his first resolution . . .

Lamb's writing commitments were discharged despite his years of unpalatable grind in the counting-house – six days a week, with a single week off in summer. When he was 50 his employers offered a pension, which allowed him a few years of freedom at the end of his life. This piece of luck provoked some sober reflections: 'That is the only true Time that a man may call his own – that which he has all to himself; the rest, though in some sense he may be said to live it, is other people's Time, not his.' But still the humour bubbles up, albeit suffused with sadness:

I am no longer clerk to the Firm of, etc. I am Retired Leisure. I am to be met with in trim gardens. I am already come to be known by my vacant face and careless gesture, perambulating at no fixed pace, nor with any settled purpose. I walk about; not to and from.

The elegant Slightly Foxed mug, much mourned (because no longer available), carried a second-hand quote from Lamb taken from the very first issue of *Slightly Foxed*: 'Charles Lamb once told Coleridge he was especially fond of books containing traces of buttered muffins.' Today Lamb is less quoted than he might have been, due in part to the complexity of his style. Still, the work contains many interesting sentiments expressed in original ways, like the eight examples below, only one of which is among the thirty-nine Lambisms in the current *Oxford Dictionary of Quotations*:

(On the convalescent) How sickness enlarges the dimensions of a man's self to himself! He is his own exclusive subject.

(On the borrower) He cometh to you with a smile and troubleth you with no receipt.

(On reading) When I am not walking, I am reading. I cannot sit and think. Books think for me.

(On newspapers) Newspapers always excite curiosity. No one ever lays one down without a feeling of disappointment.

(On poverty) There is some merit in putting a handsome face upon indigent circumstances.

(On distant correspondents) It is not easy work to set about a correspondence at our distance. The weary work of waters between us oppresses the imagination.

(On drinking) The drinking man is never less himself than during his sober intervals.

(On drinking) To mortgage miserable morrows for nights of madness . . . are the wages of buffoonery and death.

Just before Christmas 1834 Lamb fell over in Edmonton High Street. He grazed his forehead, contracted a fatal skin infection and died within the week. His sister Mary survived him by thirteen troubled years. Their joint grave is in the grounds of All Saints Church, Edmonton. Lamb's cottage – Edmonton's celebrated tourist spot – cannot have been a cheerful home for his last two years because it was actually a small, privately run madhouse where Mary was committed and where Charles went to be with her. When you peer through the front gate today the place has a rather sombre look.

I doubt whether today's batch of Edmonton schoolteachers urge their pupils – as mine did – to visit the cottage; and I very much doubt whether those pupils read *Essays of Elia*, because they are fast becoming a footnote in English literary history. Yet when reading about the Lambs I imagine the riotous evenings they presided over among their wide circle of friends and regret that Lamb did not have his own Boswell; and I still relish the quirky, uneven, funny, perceptive and inimitable style of a pre-eminent English essayist.

DAVID SPILLER lived in Edmonton for the first twenty-three years of his life and was indoctrinated into the Lambs by his primary school teacher, Marjorie Morse.

Building Jerusalem

ALISON LIGHT

I met the novelist Ruth Adler thirty years ago. She was then in her eighties, an elegant, quietly spoken but forthright woman. For a while she had been, as my husband put it, one of his many mothers. For much of his childhood during the Second World War and in the years that followed, while his own mother was working after her divorce, Raphael was parked on relatives or close friends. All of them, like Ruth Adler – the pen name of Ray Waterman – were members of the British Communist Party, the majority having joined in the 1930s. 'Party' households were not renowned for their comfort; Raphael's mother scorned domesticity as bourgeois. So he generally found himself in cheerless, spartan rooms strewn with a few utilitarian items, table and chairs piled up with pamphlets, as if awaiting a committee meeting. But Ray's house was special. Soft furnishings, pottery, paintings and, above all, the feeling of a *home*.

These memories came to mind as I read Ruth/Ray's novel *Beginning Again* (1983) for the first time recently. At its centre is Rebecca Lederman and her love for her husband, Morris, a man entirely given up to his political work. Rebecca shares and respects his views – they are both 'Bolshies' – but she also wants time to herself to write. Rebecca, Morris says, is a romantic. She would rather read Dickens than the *Daily Worker*, the Communist Party newspaper. She argues that great art is universal, not to be reduced to a political point of view. What's more she believes in beauty. Yet her writing always

---

Ruth Adler, *Beginning Again* (1983), is out of print but we can obtain second-hand copies.

comes second, or third, or fourth, because she too feels a deep debt to the past, to those who have suffered before her, whose memory must be upheld, and to those who are suffering injustice in the present. How, she asks herself, can one be a writer, selfishly scribbling away, when so much in the world is wrong?

The book opens in 1945 as the Ledermans arrive at their new house in north London. Rebecca is 35; she has been married to Morris for fourteen years and they are putting behind them his recent love affair with her best friend; her sons, who were evacuated, are about to return, and her parents, billeted in Leicester after escaping London's Blitz, are coming to live with them. It is a time of reconstruction for them and for Britain too: 'Europe was at peace, Fascism in disarray.' As communists, they want Britain to go further than the watered-down capitalism of the Labour Party. They want a transformation of the old hidebound, class-bound society, 'returning the land to the people, production for use not profit'. Only the Party, they believe, is fighting imperialism abroad and racial prejudice at home. 'In Rebecca's fantasy', a telling phrase, her comrades are 'pure in heart, the only ones engaged in the battle with evil'.

Houses in English literature have often symbolized the state of national life – think of Austen's *Mansfield Park* or Forster's *Howards End*, for example. Frequently too a house is identified with the woman who lives there, with her interior life, her dreams and dilemmas. Rebecca's house on four floors is multi-occupied, draughty and dirty; it is full of the past but far from insular. The Ledermans are one step away from their roots in Poland. Their politics are Internationalist, but Morris devotes much of his time to the Jewish Centre within the Party, working alongside refugees and immigrants.

While Rebecca and Morris look to the future and their boys happily play ping-pong and squabble over their homework, Rebecca's parents, Leah and Herschel, are adrift and bereft. Anxious and lonely, they miss the lively intimacy of their Yiddish-speaking community in the East End. They are haunted too by a more terrible loss. When

Herschel, fussy and highly strung, searches for the ring with which he always used to seal the wax on letters home to Poland, Leah taunts him: 'What for you want it now? You want to send them money to the next world? Hitler looks after them there free of charge as he did in this one.' But Herschel wants to find the ring just to look at it, to know it is there.

Without being dry or doctrinaire, and also without making fun of it, the novel captures the lost world of the British Communist Party in the late 1940s: branch meetings dominated by earnest and sometimes acrimonious discussion; hardworking cadres who live on next to nothing and spend every weekend canvassing, marching, distributing leaflets, organizing meetings or fundraising; people from across all walks of life who form study groups, to read together and debate. Rebecca's meandering thoughts – has she left the gas on at home? what is there for dinner? – and her self-analysis often provide an ironic counterpoint. Feeling pressured she volunteers to sell papers and take on donkeywork, briefly glowing, as she notes, with self-approval. Mostly, though, she burns with resentment as Morris's increasing commitments leave the domestic work to her.

Morris's faith, on the other hand, never waivers. More remarkably, the reader never ceases to like him. A large man, in every sense, overflowing with generosity and good humour, his politics are a vital part of him. Being a communist and being Jewish are for him indivisible. In Leipzig for the International Book Fair, back on hated German soil, Morris conquers his repugnance by meeting young people eager to build the new Democratic Republic. At the heart of the book is his journey to his home village. He finds only one Jewish survivor, a young woman who is now the memory of an entire community, the archive of its annihilation. She lives with the elderly Polish peasant who risked his life many times over, keeping her in the cellar under his floor for three years. Wouldn't she be better off in Warsaw with company her own age or other survivors, Morris wonders. 'I would as soon abandon my father as this old man,' she replies. Communism for Morris means creating such bonds across humanity.

Beginning Again is breathtakingly honest. Nothing in this novel is simple and no one is holier than thou. The Ledermans are landlords – 'a dirty word in the Party. As bad as bourgeoisie or shareholders'. They send their boys to a private school, albeit a local, progressive one. The Jewish family, for all the affection in the portrayal, is far from sentimentalized. Rebecca's brother, Ben, a returned soldier, is slowly being throttled by parental demands and expectations. Broken down by the war, unable to find girls physically attractive, he desperately needs to get away from those 'who'd die for him'.

Rebecca also fends off her mother, who trips downstairs from her lodgings on her tiny heels every ten minutes to interrupt her daughter, to display the fine piece of meat she has bought, or to gossip about nothing in particular. Any hint of comic or nostalgic 'Yiddishkeit' is soon dispersed by a dream in which Rebecca imagines herself walking round and round a concentration camp with her mother on her back; there are times when she wishes her mother were dead and the burden of guilt lies heavy on her shoulders.

Rebecca knows she is her own worst enemy. She is trapped by her need to create a nice home, to keep up high standards of cleaning and cooking, and to buy new things. She is constitutionally incapable of letting the housework go to pot, like her painter friend Julia; nor can she slough off family responsibilities or be like Helen, a doctor who lives alone and has 'free unions' with different men. Eventually she can afford a char, but she is only too aware that she is now shuffling part of her dirty work on to another woman. Yet when she finally escapes the house to Hampstead Heath for an hour, pen and paper at the ready, she gives herself up to the trees and the sunshine, and writes not a word.

Beginning Again won the 'Woman of the Eighties' Book award in 1983. It would certainly have chimed with the spirit of the contemporary Women's Liberation Movement, the campaign around

'Wages for Housework', for instance. But Adler's outlook belongs more to Bolshevism than to 'second-wave' feminism. When Rebecca lambasts 'all this ridiculous shopping, cooking, cleaning up and thinking about meals for each little family on its own', she imagines collective canteens and laundries. Like latter-day feminists for whom the personal was political, Rebecca and Morris believe that the inner life should be worked on too: they make love before marriage and see jealousy and possessiveness as a disfigurement, treating a person as property. But in making Rebecca's touchstones George Bernard Shaw and other free-thinkers, Adler reminds us that radical experiments in living have a long history.

Though the novel is a fictional retrospect, not reportage, Adler wisely ends it in 1949. Any later and it would become a chronicle of disillusionment as the horrors of Stalinism, already half-suspected, could no longer be denied. After the Soviet invasion of Hungary in 1956, many adherents, like Adler herself and most of her circle, left the Party. In the novel, Rebecca has to lower her sights. She accepts, though not ungrudgingly, that she cannot have everything, and that self-fulfilment is not enough of a goal. Without those prepared to fight for something beyond their own needs, women and children, she thinks, would still be down the mines and fascism would never have been beaten. Men will have to be domesticated, she decides, and she will have to work on it.

It comes as no surprise to discover that Ruth Adler was a late starter, only finding time to write after the death of her husband and her parents. She wrote two novels. The first, *A Family of Shopkeepers* (1973), vividly evokes her parents' life and her growing up in Stepney in the 1910s and '20s. Ten years later she finished its sequel, *Beginning Again*, published when she was 70. Both deserve to be reprinted.

ALISON LIGHT lives in Oxford. She has recently written *A Radical Romance*, a memoir of her marriage to her first husband, the historian Raphael Samuel, who was brought up, in his words, 'a fanatic child Communist' in Britain.

Great Gossips

CHARLES ELLIOTT

T. H. White (1906–64) was clearly a strange fellow, which should be evident to anyone who has read his books. The best known, of course, is his Arthurian epic, *The Once and Future King* (progenitor of *Camelot*), but he also wrote such memorable – and delightful – books as *Mistress Masham's Repose* (about a crew of Lilliputians who fetch up in the garden of an English estate, see *SF* no. 2), a moving account of training a goshawk, and a sort of diary about field sports and flying called *England Have My Bones*. He even translated a medieval bestiary.

If the range of his writings gives a hint of his eccentricity, his writing itself – quirky, succinct, honest and frequently funny – does the rest. White was not a happy man; he was driven and to a degree self-destructive, yet his enthusiasms and interests were unstoppable. This is why I personally treasure a couple of books out on the edge of his oeuvre, *The Age of Scandal* and *The Scandalmonger*, a pair of off-beat anthologies/commentaries on the eighteenth century that deal with what Lytton Strachey called 'the littleness underlying great events'. Probably nobody else would have put them together with quite the verve and amusement that White did.

It helped that he was by nature conservative if not hidebound, savagely opposed to most aspects of modern life. 'I believe', he writes (only slightly tongue-in-cheek), 'that the peak of British culture was reached in the latter years of George III: that the rot began to set in with the "Romantics", that the apparent prosperity of Victoria's reign

---

T. H. White, *The Age of Scandal* (1950) and *The Scandalmonger* (1952), are both out of print but we can obtain second-hand copies.

was autumnal, not vernal: and that now we are done for.' Such an attitude amply justifies his retreat into the company of those engaging and talkative chroniclers of his favourite period – Horace Walpole, Boswell, Johnson, Thomas Creevy, the wits, diarists, letter writers and gossips. The fragments he assembles here add up to nothing profound, which may be why they are so much fun.

I was in college when *The Age of Scandal* was published in 1950 (its companion, *The Scandalmonger*, came out two years later) and was so delighted by it that I decided to become an eighteenth-century scholar myself. I'm glad to report that this did not happen – I came to my senses sometime around 1954, with the US draft (that is, conscription). In the meantime, however, I rejoiced in everything eighteenth-century, from Gibbon to Stephen Duck, the Thresher Poet. I went so far as to collect Boswell's poetry for a graduate paper (don't ask – it's terrible). To this day I am happy to subscribe to White's comment that 'few people seem to realize how charming and peculiar The Age of Scandal was'.

The key to its attraction was gossip. In the palaces of royalty and the salons of the aristocracy gossip flourished, spinning off bon mots and stories which were usually disgraceful. Horace Walpole reported with feline delight the 'fracas at Kensington' when George II had his chair pulled out from under him and, 'being mortal in the part that touched the ground', quite failed to see the joke. George I, it turns out, spent much of his time in his mistress's apartment cutting up paper, while George IV convinced himself that he had commanded a division at Waterloo (he hadn't). True or not, the gossip is memorable and, among the jokes and tall tales, White offers dozens of equally memorable facts. Who would have guessed, for instance, that British soldiers used 6,500 tons of flour for powdering their hair every year? Or that officers carried umbrellas during the battles of the Peninsular War? (Wellington disapproved. 'On duty at St James's [Guards] may carry them if they please; but in the field it is not only ridiculous but unmilitary.')

If there is a hero in these books, it is Horace Walpole, the epicene son of the great politician Sir Robert Walpole (but possibly the illegitimate offspring of Alexander Pope's enemy Lord Hervey). Rich enough to be idle, Horry wrote long gossipy letters, published his own books and created a plasterwork palace at Strawberry Hill ('the little Ark with pinnacles') that led public fashion into a taste for the Gothic. The parade of human folly delighted him. Writing of the gambling craze in 1770, he describes it as 'worthy of the decline of an Empire' and reports how two gentlemen 'had made a match for five hundred pounds between five turkeys and five geese to run from Norwich to London'. Nor was that the most exotic bet. One gambling man, wagering that a human being could live under water, recruited a 'desperado', placed him in a box and submerged him. He drowned. Undaunted, the gambler recruited another, presumably with the same result.

Then there was 'bottom'. White devotes a whole chapter to this concept, which had a very different meaning in the eighteenth century from the one it has today. Bottom was a quality a gentleman was expected to have, and meant something like courage or grace under pressure. It might apply to the ability to hold one's nerve at cards or to undergo a flogging, or a willingness to out-drink another. Dr Johnson sums up the latter talent with this 'magnificent apostrophe': 'No, Sir, claret is the liquor for boys; port for men; but he who aspires to be a hero must drink brandy.' Displaying one's bottom might have tragic consequences. To prove that he had the

Acquiring 'bottom' (at Westminster School)

73

nerve to cure his hiccoughs, the famous daredevil John Mytton set his nightshirt on fire and incinerated himself.

It is tempting – and perhaps not such a bad idea – simply to browse through these books plucking out small treasures of wit or narrative. They make ideal bedtime reading. Witness, for example, the terrifying Mrs Schellenberg, an aged member of the court of George III's queen, whose German accent could 'shatter' English idioms. As Fanny Burney reports, Mrs Schellenberg had another peculiarity. She kept a pair of pet frogs. 'I can make them croak when I will,' Burney reports her saying. 'When I go so to my snuff-box, knock, knock, knock, they croak all what I please.' Dogs were considerably more common companions, and more fashionable; White notes that Mrs Thrale, 'though not particularly doggy', had about sixteen of them in the house, while 'the Marquis de Sade had a hound which conformed loyally to its master's theories: it ate six sheep and was called Dragon'.

Life could be challenging in the eighteenth century. So melodramatic was the time, 'so much the reverse of the Age of Reason . . . that the strain of living in those decades might have intimidated a cowboy', White writes.

> The heaths were sprinkled with highwaymen and gibbets, the towns patrolled by window-smashing mobs, the people of the sea-ports ready to fly from the press gangs or from the smugglers, London rich in brothels which were called *bagnios* and in gin shops where it was possible to 'get drunk for a penny or dead drunk for twopence'.

Nor did you need to be on a country lane to run into trouble. George II, while walking in the very centre of London, was confronted by a highwayman in Kensington Gardens who, 'with a manner of great deference', relieved him of his purse, his watch and his shoe buckles. The Neapolitan ambassador was robbed in Grosvenor Square. Violence, in fact, seems to have been pervasive.

Even religion had its rough edges, with class distinctions shaping sects from the Ranters ('these uneducated and generally insane enthusiasts') to the highest Anglicans. Firmness in one's faith could reach an alarming pitch. Edward Thurlow, the crusty Lord Chancellor under George III, thus addressed himself to a deputation of Nonconformists:

> I'm against you, by God. I am for the Established Church, damme! Not that I have any more regard for the Established Church than for any other church, but because it is established. And if you can get your damned religion established, I'll be for that too!

The Reverend Sydney Smith showed the same spirit. On his deathbed he complained of being so weak that 'I verily believe, if the knife were put into my hand, I should not have the strength or energy enough to stick it into a Dissenter.' The Dissenters, on the other hand, could hardly be ignored. The great Methodist John Wesley ('dismal and humourless' in White's view) preached no less than 42,400 sermons in his long career.

All this energy was hardly confined to wit and eccentricity but had a tendency to shift into actual, bloody violence as well. White, possibly to an unfortunate degree, has a taste for this. Executions, duels and general mayhem come in for considerable attention. While he points out that the duels gradually became gentrified, governed by rules of conduct so detailed that opponents 'could treat each other, even in the act of slaughter, with scrupulous good manners', it took very little to offend a noble lord. One gentleman took to his bed for six weeks after receiving a letter from a fellow peer that omitted 'very' in signing a letter to him as 'your [very] humble servant'.

There was nothing at all genteel about executions. The list of crimes for which hanging could be imposed was improbably long, and each one took place before cheering crowds of onlookers. There was even a fashion for necrophilia. Horace Walpole's creepy friend

George Selwyn achieved a dubious sort of fame for what was described as his 'passion to see coffins and corpses, and executions'. Selwyn had been sent down from Oxford for celebrating Holy Communion while pretending to be Jesus Christ. Many stories, generally gruesome, were told about him. I rather like the one about Lord Holland, on his deathbed. 'Next time Mr Selwyn calls,' Holland told his servant, 'show him up. If I am alive, I shall be delighted to see him, and if I am dead he will be delighted to see me.' Given the physical circumstances of life at the time, insouciance about death may have been necessary. 'Five of Crabbe's seven children died,' White notes; 'Gibbon was the sole survivor of seven siblings; four of Sterne's brothers died; Gray was the only one who lived, from a family of twelve.'

In a way I'm slightly embarrassed to be recommending *The Age of Scandal* and *The Scandalmonger.* After all, great matters were being decided in the second half of the eighteenth century – wars of various sizes fought, the machine age approaching, political movements underway that would change the shape of society. Important stuff, in other words, pretty much none of which touches these books as more than the faintest off-stage echo. What we get instead is history as entertainment. Still, so far as I am concerned, there is room in the world for that.

CHARLES ELLIOTT is a retired editor and the author of several books of essays.

All the World's a Stage

HELEN RICHARDSON

When I was a child, people of a certain age who met my father often remarked, 'You look just like Simon Callow.' I had no idea who Simon Callow was, so my father bought me his autobiography, *Being an Actor* (1986). Over the years it has become my battered treasure, all creased corners and cracked spine, highlighted and annotated, lent to friends and quickly sought back. Callow takes us into a singular world where the emotions and anxieties of ordinary life are exposed, examined and amplified. He offers insight into what it is to be an actor and, I would say, what it is to be human.

Callow's roles both in film (notably *Four Weddings and a Funeral*) and in theatre are too numerous to mention. But there are surely few who could step nimbly from Samuel Beckett's *Waiting for Godot* to Andrew Lloyd Webber's musical *The Woman in White*, from playing Orlando in the National Theatre's *As You Like It* to Dickens in Peter Ackroyd's one-man show *The Mystery of Charles Dickens* – as well as directing operas such as *Die Fledermaus* and *Così fan tutte*. In addition to all this he is a seductive writer.

> When I was eighteen, I wrote Laurence Olivier a letter. He replied, by return of post, inviting me to join the National Theatre company – in the box office. I accepted immediately, and as I crossed the foyer to be interviewed by the box office manager, I thought, crystal clear and without any sense of destiny about it: 'One day I shall run this place.'

Simon Callow, *Being an Actor* (1986)

Vintage · Pb · 400pp · £10.99 · ISBN 9780099471950

The essence of Callow is contained in that one little paragraph: first, in the way he skips over the fact that even as an 18-year-old his writing had the power to catch the attention of Laurence Olivier. What was in that letter? He never says. Second is his ability to create a theatrical moment as the young Callow crosses the foyer towards his future. Third is his honesty – not many of us would admit to the ambitions that our teenage selves dared to entertain.

Essentially *Being an Actor* is a detailed study of the two sides of creativity, a study that is applied here to the theatre but which can be applied to all types of creative output: one side is flair, art and instinct; the other is painstaking craft, failure and determination. The first is glamorous and sparkling – the face that everybody sees. The latter is craven, self-doubting and difficult – the face that you see in the mirror.

Callow describes appearing, as a drama student in Dublin, in a 'monstrous' production of Chekhov's *The Seagull*, adjudicated by one of his heroes, Micheál Mac Liammóir.

> As for me, I was appalling. The earth opened up under my feet every time I stepped on stage. It was a shallow, nasty piece of work. I didn't know what I was doing, while at the same time knowing all too well. By now, I had become an avid theatregoer, and I knew what was good. This was not.

Mac Liammóir's damning assessment of Callow was that he was not a natural.

> 'Micheál,' I said to him afterwards, 'you said I was not a born actor.'
>
> 'Ah, but you could *become* one,' he replied.

Callow sets out on an intense period of study and preparation. He shadows Mac Liammóir backstage. He begins to engage with the question: *Who am I?* And he leaves university in Dublin, moves back to London, auditions for the Drama Centre, and is offered a place. There follow years of being broken down, dissected and criti-cized by his teachers, tormented by anxiety and self-doubt.

Then, one night on stage, he lets go. 'I had no time to think about my performance . . . I just did it. Suddenly, for the first time, I was acting. Not performing, or posturing, or puppeteering. *I was being another way.*' This is the moment when Mac Liammóir's idea, that with enough training one can be reborn, finally begins to make sense. 'It was then, in that moment, that acting became second nature to me.'

Becoming an Actor is a startlingly honest book, a self-portrait of the actor, neuroses and all, from his first reactions to drama school – 'It is not too late to leave. Everyone is better than I am . . . I must be mad to have come here at all' – to the experience of feeling itchy and claustrophobic inside his own skin:

> I was, in fact, in a state of continuous torment. I hated myself for my cowardice, for not having lived . . . I had long and ter-rifying periods of utter blankness, feeling nothing. I tried to write, to paint. No go. I couldn't find a crack in the wall of my personality through which to escape.

For Callow these excursions into the murkier parts of his psyche are his most powerful fuel, his engine for improvement: 'Through it all, I was sustained by an enormous strength: I knew how bad I was. Had I thought that I was any good, I would have been lost.'

As well as exposing the nuts and bolts of the theatre, bringing that world to life in a way that is compelling for an outsider, *Being an Actor* is an attempt to unpick the method, to explain the magic of the 'perfect performance'. Yet in the end, Callow remains as baffled as he ever was by those lucid moments where everything just works, as in his 1985 role as Molina in *The Kiss of the Spiderwoman*:

> I proceeded to give the best performance of anything I have ever given in my life . . . This has happened so rarely in my

career that it is worth drawing special attention to it. It is a real mystery . . . It seems deeply immodest of me to speak like this, but it is the opposite, because I can claim no credit for it . . . It all leaped out of me, fully formed.

Being an Actor evolved from a speech Callow gave at Goldsmiths College entitled 'The Actor as a Paradigm of the Human Condition'. Though rather tongue-in-cheek, it seems apt. The process of discovering who we are is often a series of performances of who we believe ourselves to be. We try out different characters, discover and test the various aspects of who we might become as we settle into our own skin. Actors are made acutely aware of their progress on that journey every time they take to the stage.

We are all inwardly aware of the unnerving gap between our secret insecurities and our outer shell, and perhaps actors feel this even more keenly. Being an actor requires you to present yourself with total assurance and confidence, all the while knowing that you are a half-formed thing.

In his preface, Callow writes that the book will have served its purpose if people outside the theatre world read it and think, 'Oh *that's* what it's like to be an actor.' As a non-actor and occasional theatregoer I have read and reread it many times, and I have thought over and over again, 'That's what it's like to *be*.'

HELEN RICHARDSON writes fiction and poetry, and is a producer of documentary films and commercials. Her first novel, *Waking*, was published in 2017.

Joan's Books

A. F. HARROLD

A little while ago I was visiting a school. As a children's author and poet this is one of the things I do regularly in order (a) to keep in touch with young people and (b) to pay the rent. In this instance I was at my partner's alma mater, a small boarding school in Oxford called Wychwood.

While I was there I told all the teachers I met of the exciting fact I had recently discovered, which was that their school had been an early pre-war home to the then pupil, and future writer, Joan Aiken. Some teachers knew this, and some were surprised to learn it, but the reaction common to all was that Wychwood had always encouraged individuality and personality in the girls (my partner's a stand-up comedian and podcaster, so it worked there). It certainly seems to have been the case for Aiken, that most various of authors.

Joan Aiken was the daughter of the American poet laureate Conrad Aiken and the Canadian writer Jessie MacDonald, and two of her siblings also wrote books, so writing clearly ran in the family. From her pen came a raft of books, including a handful of Jane Austen sequels, period romances, supernatural short stories and most things in between. What I want to write about here though is her sequence of eleven novels for children that began with *The Wolves of Willoughby*

Joan Aiken's sequence of novels for children comprises *The Wolves of Willoughby Chase* (1962); *Black Hearts in Battersea* (1964); *Nightbirds on Nantucket* (1966); *The Stolen Lake* (1981); *Limbo Lodge* (1999); *The Cuckoo Tree* (1971); *Dido and Pa* (1986); *Is* (1992); *Cold Shoulder Road* (1995); *Midwinter Nightingale* (2003); and *The Witch of Clatteringshaws* (2005). Most of them are are available in paperback in Random House's Red Fox imprint.

Chase in 1962 – page-turning adventure stories, set in a mostly historical past, with a sprinkling of the paranormal and a bucketful of brilliant characters.

The Wolves of Willoughby Chase begins, conventionally enough, in 1832, with a girl called Bonnie Green meeting her grotesque and bony new governess, Miss Slighcarp, who informs her that her parents have died in a shipwreck and that she is now an orphan. So far, so standard. However, the 1832 of the book is not the 1832 of our history. We are told, in a brief preface, that King James III has recently ascended the throne and a harsh winter on the Continent has driven wolves north, through the Channel Tunnel, into England.

And so, in the second chapter we meet Sylvia, who is put on a train and sent off to visit her cousin Bonnie at Willoughby Chase. An uncomfortable scene unfolds as she is offered sweets and pastries by a fellow traveller, a man with endless boxes, it seems, of sweets and pastries. After a while the train slows and stops and a wolf crashes through their carriage window. The man smothers it with his coat and stabs it in the throat with a shard of broken glass.

> 'Tush,' said Sylvia's companion, breathing heavily and passing his hand over his face. 'Unexpected – most.'
>
> He extracted the dead wolf from the folds of the cloak and tipped its body, with some exertion, out through the broken window. There was a chorus of snarling and yelping outside, and then the wolves seemed to take fright at the appearance of their dead comrade, for Sylvia saw them coursing away over the snow.

I must admit that the first time I read this I was shocked. I hadn't been expecting such brutal slaughter in only the second chapter, and so casually described and dealt with. Clearly we were not in Kansas . . .

Pat Marriott

The plot of the book is the usual 'orphans betrayed by a wicked governess and sold to a workhouse' sort of thing, and it all comes right by the end, mostly, but what makes it really special is what happens afterwards . . . in the next book.

Black Hearts in Battersea (1965) sees the goose-boy, Simon, who helped Bonnie and Sylvia win the day in the first book, make his way to London, where he wants to study art at Furneaux's Academy. He lodges with the Twite family who, it turns out, are Hanoverian plotters, intending to blow up the Jacobite king. The plot is foiled, but Battersea Castle is destroyed and the youngest Twite daughter, Dido (who is not as bad as her terrorist father), is lost at sea . . . only to be rescued by whalers and taken to Nantucket in *Nightbirds on Nantucket* (1966). This is where the series really gets into its stride because with Dido, Aiken had found the heroine she wanted.

A precursor, perhaps, of Philip Pullman's Lyra, Dido Twite is an irrepressible, curious trouble-finder (rather than troublemaker), funny, fearless and faithful. She's the star of many of the following novels, and it's clear that Aiken found her a wonderful foil, since twice in future years she went back and added Dido novels into the series – *The Stolen Lake* (1981) and *Limbo Lodge* (1999). Both books recount adventures that fit chronologically between Dido's being washed up in Nantucket and making it back to England in *The Cuckoo Tree* (1971).

I particularly loved *The Stolen Lake* with its supernatural elements, its terrifying child-snatching witches and the wonder of its South American Celtic colony, New Cumbria, founded in the fifth century AD by King Arthur.

Throughout the series, and its alternative history, the adventures are strange and beautiful and moving – Aiken really feels for her heroes and heroines, children lost in a maze of unfairness, tragedy, comedy and politics, battling grown-ups and wolves (and werewolves and witches) as well as themselves. We re-encounter Dido's father (in *Dido and Pa*, 1986), an itinerant hoboy, or oboe player, who, when reunited with his daughter, proves himself to be a complete dastard (though capable of making the most beautiful, soulful music).

> And he never, never once played for me. And oh, his music was so sweet! There was a tune I called 'Calico Alley', acos of the words I put to it, 'As I went dancing down Calico Alley'; and the one that went to 'Three Herrings for a Ha'penny'; and the one I called 'Black Cat Coming Down Stairs', because it sounded so solemn; and the one I thought was about rain, quick and tinkly. But the best of 'em all was 'Oh, how I'd like to be queen, Pa'.

We also meet Dido's half-sister, Is, locked in the basement and brutalized, and we whimper with the shame of it, the smallness of her, so similar to the Dido we first met many books earlier, but oh how Dido has grown and come into her own . . . There is hope, even in the darkness.

The *Wolves* books run like a golden thread through Aiken's writing life, as she comes back to them again and again, even while she's writing so many other books, in so many other registers and for so many other audiences, so much so that the final volume, *The Witch of Clatteringshaws*, was published posthumously as her last book in 2005.

The Witch of Clatteringshaws reminds me, in a sideways way, of Iris Murdoch's last book, *Jackson's Dilemma*, in that both are shorter than their preceding books, and both are slightly mysterious (or, to be less generous, muddled – Murdoch's being muddled by Alzheimer's, of course, but still a book to reread).

Heartbreakingly, Aiken includes an afterword in her last book, admitting as much: 'I knew it was going to have to be a short book, as I am growing old and didn't have the energy for a long one. But I knew it would be better to write a short book than get stuck in the middle of a long one and fail to finish it.' (She had a go, she says, at finishing Austen's unfinished *The Watsons*, but it's just not the same . . .) 'My loving publishers went along with this arrangement, but, just the same, they said, when the manuscript was delivered, they *would* like a few things explained.' She explains a few things, and then: 'The end came too quickly, said the editors. Yes, it did, and I apologize. But a speedy end is better than a half-finished story.'

She gets Dido and Simon, the two mainstays of the series, free, by the end of the novel, of the responsibilities they'd come into during the previous books, responsibilities that tied their hands, that constrained their freedom. Since the children had grown up across the books, and had been thrown together and pulled apart so often, Aiken got them to a position where 'Dido [is] free to marry him if she chooses', and it's this freedom that I find so invigorating – not only is it Dido's choice, not Simon's (who asked her once before), but it's also not Aiken's choice . . . truly she sets her characters free at the end, beyond the back cover, off the stage, away in their own lives, lived beyond the reader's gaze.

If I were to write books with half the verve and heart that the *Wolves* sequence has, if I could create characters with half the energy and passion that Dido has, if I could think of a third 'if I could' to complete this trio of wishful comparisons, I'd be a happy children's writer. Still, I try, and Dido and Joan are lighting the way ahead for me, and when I stumble, it's not their fault, but when I get it right, I acknowledge the debt I owe to them.

And now to finish with an admission. The *Wolves* books are all I have read of Aiken, but now I feel I am standing on the edge of a rabbit hole down which I'm about to fall . . . there are so many more books by her to explore, the world is so rich with undiscovered treasure, and, like Dido, I intend to discover it.

A. F. HARROLD was born and grew up in Sussex, not a million miles from where Joan Aiken settled, but left there half a lifetime ago. He now lives in Reading where he makes books and poems for children.

Perilous Times

PATRICK WELLAND

In the summer of 1974, the author Olivia Manning reread the transcript of a BBC radio talk she had given eleven years earlier about her arrival in Cairo in 1941 with her husband, Reggie Smith. Although she was not well, it inspired her to follow her Balkan trilogy (see *SF* no. 63), detailing the wartime experiences of Harriet and Guy Pringle in Bucharest and Athens, with a second sequence set in Egypt and the Middle East. The task took five years and by the time it was finished Manning had only months to live. She died in July 1980, aged 72.

She made no secret of the fact that the Balkan trilogy was strongly autobiographical, both in its dissection of an English community living under the threat of German invasion and its depiction of a marriage under strain. Like Manning, Harriet is newly married to a man whose gregarious spirit leads him to embrace others, to her emotional exclusion. By the close of the first sequence, however, she acknowledges that the perils of war have forced them to a mutual understanding and that the only certainty left to them is to stay together.

The Levant trilogy is no less a seamless fusion of historical fact and imaginative fiction. It is June 1942 and the Pringles have fled Romania and Greece one step ahead of the Nazis. Now, settled in Cairo, they are again under threat as Rommel's Afrika Corps drives remorselessly east following its successes in Libya.

Olivia Manning's Levant trilogy, *The Danger Tree* (1977), *The Battle Lost and Won* (1978) and *The Sum of Things* (1980), is available as a single-volume paperback: Weidenfeld & Nicolson · 576pp · £12.99 · ISBN 9780753808184. Readers may also enjoy Deirdre David's absorbing biography, *Olivia Manning: A Woman at War* (OUP, 2013).

These are catastrophic times. Tobruk has fallen, the British are in retreat, abandoning weaponry and tanks, and it is rumoured Cairo is to be evacuated. Determined to evoke not just the fears of civilians on the periphery of fighting but also the horror of combat itself, Manning introduces in the opening book, *The Danger Tree*, a gauche young officer, Simon Boulderstone, through whose eyes we witness the ultimately successful El Alamein campaign.

Manning could write from experience about the hardships of living in wartime Bucharest and Athens, but she had to rely on outside sources for her description of the frontline desert war. Scrupulous, she consulted military experts and immersed herself in the recollections, published and oral, of participants. The result is an utterly convincing evocation of bloodshed and endurance that we feel could have been written by one who was there.

Here is the 'supreme awfulness' of an artillery barrage, the intensity of which reduces men to a state of collapse; the 'stench of death that came on the wind'; sun-bleached skeletons stripped bare by local Arabs; soldiers dying as their blood drains into the sand; burned-out tanks standing like 'disabled crows'; and, above all, the terrible unforgiving desert, the men 'breathing sand, eating sand, blinded and deafened by sand'.

> Two tanks stood in the middle distance . . . a man was standing in one of the turrets motionless, as though unaware of Simon's approach. Simon stopped at a few yards' distance to observe the figure, then saw it was not a man. It was a man-shaped cylinder that faced him with white and perfect teeth set in a charred black skull. He could make out the eye sockets and the triangle that had once supported a nose . . .

Manning rightly resented the description of 'woman writer' with its patronizing implication that women cannot write authoritatively about men: 'There is no inherent reason why men should be mysteries to women and beyond their power to treat convincingly in a novel, or vice versa.' Even so, her talent for entering the male psyche is exceptional.

As the desert claims its dead, so the melting-pot of Cairo disturbs the living. Away from battle, it forms the backdrop to both *The Danger Tree* and its successor, *The Battle Lost and Won*. Manning – who recalled Cairo as 'the final bolthole of Europe' – disliked the baking city with its flies, beggars and disease. But in her hands it has an almost human presence: its streets are 'coagulated by heat' which sticks to the skin like cotton wool; its 'spicy, flaccid atmosphere' is pierced by the rancid smell of human waste; its men in white robes flicker through the gloom or hang 'like a swarm of bees' from tram doors; a mosque squats like a 'fat white watchful cat'.

Here again war has thrown together a disparate English colony of the privileged, the dutiful and the cowardly, beset by uncertainty and rumour and killing time with heavy drinking and transient affairs. Harriet's friend Lady Angela Hooper, stricken by grief at her young son's death from a stick bomb, buries her misery by indulging an infatuation for the boozy poet and journalist Bill Castlebar. The man-eating Edwina Little seeks solace in the untrustworthy arms of a married officer. Both relationships reflect the coarsening amorality engendered by war.

It becomes ever clearer that Guy, employed by the British Council, does not want a private life. He cannot understand that 'his desire to embrace the outside world was an infidelity and an indulgence'. Harriet, given more freedom than she originally wanted, explores increasing independence and her tone becomes more critical and detached.

This criticism extends to the British imperial mission with which Manning, resenting the assumption of cultural superiority embedded in the idea of the Council, was disenchanted. Harriet watches disdainfully at the Anglo-Egyptian Union club as English officers deride the 'gyppos' in obscene songs, while a group of English abase themselves at a live sex show in Cairo's seedy Berka district.

In contrast, Harriet's elegant Egyptian doctor Shafik treats her with impeccable old-world courtesy, while saying with gentle irony, 'Could we let a member of your great empire die here, in this poor country?' Surely, says Simon, Britain has brought Egypt only 'justice and prosperity'. Harriet replies: 'What have we done here, except make money . . . the real people of the country . . . are just as diseased, underfed and wretched as they ever were.'

Familiar figures emerge from the past. Gracey, head of the Council who had been living in decadent splendour as the guest of a wealthy Turk, escapes to Palestine. At the British Embassy the diplomat Dobson joins staff in feeding papers into a bonfire. The odious, and ultimately doomed, Lord Pinkrose reappears. Guy suggests that Harriet, in increasing ill health, join a boat bound for England. She crushes the idea but is left suspecting that he merely wants her out of the way.

When Angela leaves for Beirut with Castlebar, Harriet, recovering from amoebic dysentery, grudgingly decides to take up Guy's suggestion and sets out to board the refugee ship *Queen of Sparta*. Queuing at the gangway, full of nameless foreboding about the forthcoming voyage, she decides on impulse to join a servicewoman and her lesbian friend on a routine lorry run to Iraq via Syria. We leave her bumping across the Sinai desert, properly independent for the first time since her marriage and carefree at the thought of all the 'wonders of the Levant' on the other side of the sands. A coda records that a week after sailing, the *Queen of Sparta* was torpedoed with the loss of all on board apart from a lifeboat packed with women and children, whose fate is unknown.

Manning completed her closing book, *The Sum of Things*, in 1979 more than thirty years after the end of the war. By this time, she was assured of her place in the literary firmament although she remained typically insecure about her reputation. Since the war, she had been blighted by ill health. In 1944, she had delivered a child two months after the foetus had died in utero – a traumatic experience from which she never fully recovered – and in the following years she had surgery for various conditions, which led to bouts of depression. A lifetime of writing was drawing to its close.

The book opens with Simon, injured by a mine which kills his young driver, lying in hospital at Helwan paralysed from the waist down. Meanwhile Harriet, dropped off in wintertime Damascus, finds herself alone. Settling into a pension and thinking that Guy believes her to be at sea for the next two months, she aimlessly walks the rain-sodden streets, missing Cairo's sumptuous sunsets and moonlight like 'liquid silver'.

She finds temporary employment with the self-centred Italian Egyptologist Dr Beltado and is befriended by a gentle Syrian, Halal. As a solitary woman in a strange land she has survived. But recognizing that her attempt to live an independent life is reducing her to penury, she decides to join Angela and travels by train and taxi to Beirut where she is welcomed by her old friend and Angela's lover, Castlebar. Together, they move on to Jerusalem, Harriet still blithely unaware that Guy thinks she is dead.

Back in Cairo, with the proximity of war receding as the Allies advance, Guy, believing Harriet to have gone down with the *Queen of Sparta*, is haunted by her loss and the belated knowledge that he both ignored her needs and instigated her departure. Finally admitting the futility of his job in a reserved occupation projecting an idea of empire in which neither he nor his students believe, he recognizes that he has sacrificed the permanence of a marital relationship to needless work and the transient company of friends: 'this had been as good as any, yet he had not known it at the time'.

Harriet's moment of truth arrives when she runs into an Englishwoman at the Church of the Holy Sepulchre in Jerusalem and learns that only she and two sailors survived from the torpedoed *Queen of Sparta*, and that the ship's loss was covered in the Egyptian press. Realizing that Guy thinks she is dead, she returns to Cairo for an emotional reunion.

And so the curtain on the two trilogies is lowered. We leave Harriet and Guy in Alexandria. On their way there, Harriet, once an emotional idealist, is comforted by a realism born of harsh gestation: 'In an imperfect world marriage was a matter of making do with what one had chosen. As this thought came into her head, she pressed Guy's knee and he patted her hand again.' We know Harriet and Guy will never part. As throughout, fiction mirrored life. Despite their differences, Manning and Reggie stayed together to the end, bound by a mutual respect cemented by shared wartime suffering.

If Manning was criticized – even mocked – for seeming to hold a grudge against the world, then perhaps she can be excused. Denied her mother's love, she doggedly transcended her unpromising background, was grievously scarred by the loss of a child and endured years of ill health. Given this, her achievement is all the more remarkable. There can be few works of modern fiction in which such a large cast of characters is handled so deftly and the privations and violence of war are so neatly fused with the uncertainties of private life. Manning's often austere prose reflects a critical eye in keeping with the author's spiky personality, but the overwhelming impression is of genuine compassion for ordinary men and women coping with extraordinary and perilous times.

> Then at last peace, precarious peace, came down upon the world and the survivors could go home. Like the stray figures left on the stage at the end of a great tragedy, they had now to tidy up the ruins of war and in their hearts bury their noble dead.

After 42 years in newspapers, PATRICK WELLAND now hides from social media in Sussex.

Slightly Foxed: or, the Widower of Bayswater

WILLIAM PLOMER

Decades ago wits, poets and dukes
Circled like planets round Gloria Jukes,
Bluestocking, tuft-hunter, *grande amoureuse* –
Was ever a salon brilliant as hers?

Her name still turns up though she's turned up her toes,
You meet her in memoirs, they still quote her *mots*,
And old crones remember her faults and her furs –
Such foibles, my dear, such sables were hers!

A wrecker of homes and a breaker of hearts
She talked like a book and encouraged the arts,
Political hostesses envied her poise,
And said they preferred conversation to noise.

Her cook was a dream, her pearls were in ropes,
She furthered ambitions, she realized hopes,
Lent Dowson a fiver, put rouge on her eyebrows,
Enchanted grandees and reconciled highbrows,

Acclimatized novel Bohemian behaviour
In the stuffiest house in Victorian Belgravia,
And when St John's Wood was abandoned to orgies
Behaved like a dignified bride at St George's.

A Personage paid to her regal poitrine
A compliment royal, and she looked like a queen –
But of some Ruritanian kingdom, maybe –
All plastered with gifts like a Christmas tree.

When her guests were awash with champagne and with gin
She was recklessly sober, as sharp as a pin:
An abstemious man would reel at her look
As she rolled a bright eye and praised his last book.

She twitted George Moore, she flirted with Tree,
Gave dear Rider Haggard material for *She*,
Talked scansion with Bridges and scandal with Wilde,
To Drinkwater drank and at Crackanthorpe smiled.

Brzeska and Brooke were among those she knew,
And she lived long enough to meet Lawrences too,
D. H. and T. E. – she, who'd known R. L. S.,
Talked to Hardy of *Kim*, and to Kipling of *Tess*!

Now she's been dead for more than ten years
We look round in vain to discover her peers;
The Gloria (it has often been said) is departed
And a new, and inferior period has started . . .

But tucked right away in a Bayswater attic,
Arthritic, ignoble, stone-deaf and rheumatic,
There still lingers on, by the strangest of flukes,
Yes, Gloria's husband – Plantagenet Jukes!

Ignored in her lifetime,
He paid for her fun,
And enjoyed all the fuss.
When she died he was done.

He sold up the house and retired from the scene
Where nobody noticed that he'd ever been.
His memoirs unwritten (though once he began 'em)
He lives on a hundred and fifty per annum

And once in the day totters out for a stroll
To purchase two eggs, *The Times*, and a roll.
Up to now he has paid for his pleasures and needs
With books he had saved and that everyone reads,

Signed copies presented by authors to Gloria
In the reigns of King Edward and good Queen Victoria.
They brought in fair prices but came to an end,
Then Jukes was reduced to one book-loving friend,

A girl of the streets with a smatter of culture
And the genial ways of an African vulture.
To this bird he offered the last of the lot,
A volume of Flecker beginning to rot.

She opened it, stormed: 'Cor blimey, you're potty!
D'you think I can't see that the pages are spotty!
Your Flecker is foxed, you old fool, and I'm through!'
Then out of the door in a tantrum she flew,

Leaving poor Jukes, in the black-out, in bed
With his past, and the book, and a bruise on his head.

William Plomer (1903–73), from *Collected Poems* (1960).
Reproduced courtesy of the William Plomer Trust

Daniel Macklin

Bibliography

Ruth Adler, *Beginning Again* 66

Joan Aiken, *The Wolves of Willoughby Chase* series of children's books 81

Elizabeth Bowen, *The Death of the Heart* 40

Caryl Brahms & S. J. Simon, *Don't, Mr Disraeli!*; *No Bed for Bacon* 23

Simon Callow, *Being an Actor* 77

Fanny Cradock, *Coping with Christmas* 34

Roald Dahl, *Going Solo* 13

Joyce Grenfell, *Joyce Grenfell Requests the Pleasure* 7

Patrick Hamilton, *The Slaves of Solitude* 18

Joseph Kessel, *The Crew* 56

Charles Lamb, *Essays of Elia* 60

Olivia Manning, The Levant trilogy: *The Danger Tree*; *The Battle Lost and Won*; *The Sum of Things* 86

William Plomer, 'Slightly Foxed: or, the Widower of Bayswater' 92

James Sutherland (ed.), *The Oxford Book of Literary Anecdotes* 51

Rose Tremain, *Restoration*; *Merivel: A Man of His Time*; *The Gustav Sonata*; *Rosie* 46

T. H. White, *The Age of Scandal*; *The Scandalmonger* 71

Gordon Williams, *From Scenes Like These* 29

Coming attractions

POLLY DEVLIN goes to Hollywood · ANTHONY WELLS marvels at Montaigne · URSULA BUCHAN remembers a groundbreaking gardener · DAVID GILMOUR travels east with Somerset Maugham · ANN KENNEDY SMITH shares a spinster's lonely passion · JON WOOLCOTT listens for voices in the hall · LAURENCE SCOTT smokes a Pipe of Peace · KATE MORGAN discovers a missing letter · DAN WORSLEY meets a shrewd medieval merchant · MARTIN SORRELL goes full steam ahead